T0147839

listening to your iGod

Beginning the Climb back to Eden.

tyler James (t.J.)

iUniverse, Inc.
Bloomington

iUniverse books may be ordered through booksellers or by contacting:

iUniverse
1663 Liberty Drive
Bloomington, IN 47403
www.iuniverse.com
1-800-Authors (1-800-288-4677)

ISBN: 978-1-4502-9882-7 (sc)
ISBN: 978-1-4620-1690-7 (hc)
ISBN: 978-1-4502-9883-4 (e)

Printed in the United States of America

iUniverse rev. date: 05/02/2011

Dedicated to all Weirdkind.

Made for **<u>Our</u>** Brother Jesus and
<u>Our</u> Father, God.

Triangle of My Faith:

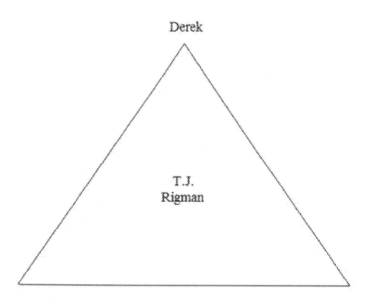

Miss you guys with all my heart. Hope I'm
doing you guys proud by writing this.

Table of Contents

"It's time to Wake your Mind up Aite. | It's time to make your mind up Aite."

-*Scott Mescudi a.k.a Kid Cudi*

Our Omniscient God

A theologian will tell you that God is the Alpha and the Omega. God has always been and always will be there. He is **Omniscient**, which by definition means "having complete or unlimited knowledge, awareness, or understanding; perceiving all things." Theologians also must agree that from the Bible we have learned that **everyone** and **everything** comes from Him. That means that any piece of knowledge or any ability, no matter if it is pleasing in his eyes or evil, this knowledge along with every other type of knowledge came from 1 Omniscient Being and we call him God.

A physicist will tell you that Energy is what makes up **Atoms** which in turn makeup all of the matter and **everything** in the Universe. A physicist will also tell you that Energy has always been and always will be, can't be created or destroyed (Alpha and Omega). So this means that **everyone** and **everything** is made up of Energy.

These definitions are the exact same just with different names. If we compare the 2 and agree that they each are very similar, the thought of Energy seems more farfetched than the thought of God. I agree that energy has always been there but it doesn't have a "beginning source" or Creator you could say. So if you think about God as **Omniscient**, which means an infinite amount of Energy, knowledge, etc… (You name it). So doesn't giving Energy a "Creator" (beginning or "birth", you could say) and giving

1

the Creator a tool to use to make us and the Universe make more sense than separating the 2 which nearly mirror each other?

Isaac Newton himself believed that God's lessons are taught through music, literature, art, and nature (Not just in the Bible).

"The knowledge of Good and Evil" is having the awareness or understanding that **any type of knowledge** can be used for Good or Evil. Everything we do is supposed to glorify God. This is because **Everything** comes from Him and we should be thanking him for the ability alone to think about and understand whatever it is we are doing; whether it be learning to draw with crayons, learning math, learning magic tricks, playing video games, learning to play the piano, or learning the Bible. **We forget to thank Him for allowing us to have the ability to learn**. So yes, of course Science and Her Laws came from Him. This book is meant to be a defense for God and Science and how God used Science and Her laws to create Us and the Universe. I view God's use of Science and His use of Earth as, you could say, our literal Mother. This lesson of our Mom (Earth) is the lesson of the **Holy Spirit** that God and Mankind have been waiting for. This lesson was taught to Us by Jesus and not a whole lot of people understood or learned the lesson. So thank you Jesus for showing us how to properly use the Power of Knowledge for Good and not for evil.

No matter who you are or what you believe in, Our Earth and Universe is governed by Laws. You may full heartedly **believe** in God and also **believe** that Science is the Devil; yet, if you fall off your porch or if you fall off the top of the building the Law of Gravity is still going to pull you down and make you fall (so after the fall do you become an atheist because God didn't "Save" you from the fall? Just a thought). Even though you don't **believe** or like Science, 1 of Science's laws is still going to "get you". The way I see it now is that the Laws of the Universe, the Universe itself, and Earth is our Mother.

Just like our birth parents. A Son knows that his Father is the only one to Fear in times of punishment, because our Mother's are more fragile and weak and we could easily over power them. Yet, we must respect what they have to say because if we do not respect what our Mother's say they will notify the Father who will punish us according to how severe the disobedience was. This could be anything from physical injury to a simple, "Hey now son." Either way, Fear and respect is given to both Dad and Mom, the power stemming from the Father. Because she is his wife she is granted equal power and respect from their children. In times of stress, sadness, anger, punishment, etc… if too much power and dependence is left on the Mom in these times with little or no guidance from the Father the child will develop a weak mind leading to all of the Abnormalities that we see today. The sight of power, fear, and respect must never be forgotten in the Father or else the child will end up being weak with Abnormalities. The last wrinkle that Man has trouble with when it comes to God is Women and why they never are mentioned of much importance to God. Guys struggling with this ask yourselves, "can I make a child without the help of a woman?" The Old Testament was the last time we Saw "Mom and Dad" working together on the same page. All of God's plagues and ways of punishment were through ways of Nature (Mom). But now that we see nature performing acts that seem random, we can say that "Mom and Dad aren't working together"; we have given more Fear to the thought of Our Mother, rather than to our Father.

Just like with the Laws of the Universe ("Science Laws"). Power and Respect is given to them (Our Mom) through the Father because he is where all of this knowledge stems from. These "Laws" of Science dictate our physical bodies here on Earth but from the Bible we know that "The Flesh" doesn't matter and the only thing that truly matters is getting into Heaven or Not. So yes, you may fall off the roof and splatter on the ground.

You fall because that's what the Father said would happen if you did that. The Mother (Earth) is only making sure those rules are followed through. After that the **Judgment** (or punishment) is left up to the Father who has now given the power of **Judgment** to His Son, Our Brother Jesus. So really we need to respect and fear the laws of our mother just so we won't do stupid things like jumping off of buildings. But, the ultimate fear and respect of the coming punishment (after Our lies, sex, drugs, video games, school, sports, most of all after your death) should come after Our Mom (Earth) reports what has happened (on her/in her) to the Father. Our fear should begin by Fearing the punishment Our Father will send his Son Jesus to follow through with. God understands now that too much power and respect has been given to Science and Mother Earth (Moms in general) and not enough anymore is given to Him and Jesus.

God isn't trying to say forget about the Laws of Science and don't respect and love your mothers. Jesus is known to be the "**Greatest Teacher**" to ever walk this planet; even atheists will give Jesus credit for that. Jesus not only taught Us how we should truly live our lives; he taught God, Our Father, that He must show **compassion** and understanding for his Children (Just like our Mom's (Mother Earth) have shown us). This makes sense when we think about how we grow here. Times always change, we all get the stories about, "back in my day we didn't have rap or all we had to do was hit a ball back and forth (Pong). I'm just saying that yes, Our Father's always are more powerful than Us but, they don't understand that times change, and more complex things develop. **They don't have the knowledge (or Understanding) of Our current generation the way that we do**. I know my Dad will come in and watch me play Call of Duty. He is interested and thinks it looks cool but he can't play for the life of himself haha. We have to meet Our parents half way to understand and appreciate what they appreciate; they too must meet us halfway and understand and appreciate what we appreciate, but we must never lose sight of the Fear and Respect we have for them. We all (including God and Jesus) need to have an understanding of what makes this Earth work. We need to show God that Mankind has gratefully and progressively gathered all of these different types and forms of knowledge and abilities from His **Omniscient collection of knowledge**. Mankind has just acted like impatient little kids breaking into Dad's library, learning and doing everything found in Dad's collection. God is very happy that we have discovered all of this knowledge but just wants us to slow down, take a step back, understand and most of all, be thankful and appreciative that all of it came from and comes from Him and his Good grace (His "Library").

Jesus came here to show Us and God that We (Mankind) can be the most powerful, knowledgeable being in the Universe and still humble ourselves and use the power of knowledge to be a force of Good for God here on Earth, and not just use that knowledge and power for our own selfish desires. It is time to take Our Brother Jesus' example/lessons serious and follow down his path to teach (show) God and each other that with His (God's) knowledge (whatever it may be) we can be a force of Good for Him, Jesus, Mom (Earth), and Each other.

You know what you are talented at and desire above all else; so if you want to be a musician or sports star, honor God and your Parents through whatever it is you do. It is your life and you need to decide what it is you want your life to do for yourself, your parents, but most of all for God and Jesus in their name. Make sure that it is not something that will go against God's word in the Bible. As long as what you want to do lines up with God and the Bible you can do it. If you're parents are against it, like mine were against me writing this book, but you know its right (Good) between you and God. Then you find strength in God who then will give you strength to accomplish the task he has given you. Eventually you will prove to your parents that you are doing the right thing for yourself and for God. But, you also must remember that no matter how "successful" or "powerful" you get or don't get, without your Mom, Dad, and God you would/will be nothing! You wouldn't exist! So no matter what you do, glorify your parents and God through it. Because whatever we do or feel like we are being called to do is all out of the **Pursuit of Our Own (Selfish) Happiness**. If we can keep all of them (Parents, God, and Jesus) then we won't have any stress or guilt for what we do and can keep a clear mind to keep them and ourselves happy. Don't concern yourself with "making your friends happy". They will see your positive (+) energy and try and deter it out of jealous. Develop a thick skin (good defensive Conscious mind) and nothing will faze you. If you are wondering why I didn't mention keeping Mother Earth happy, trust me, when the Father (God) and Jesus are happy, she is happy.

Just like domino's pizza is taking time to **show**/**teach** people that they aren't just shelling out micro-waved pizzas; I'm taking my own personal time out to try and **show**/**teach** people that all of sources of Knowledge and Happiness come from God the Father, Jesus, and the Holy Spirit (Mom). Because even if we won't admit it we are nothing without our parents; and are nothing without Dad (God) and Jesus. **Individually, we combine to make the Holy Spirit**. So when you think about the concept of the Father, the Son, and the Holy Spirit think about a Golf Bag. You are the Golf Bag. If you set the bag upright, with all of the clubs in it, alone it will not be able to stand or stand for very long. So to keep a Golf Bag standing up, it is given 2 legs to lean back on for support. **We All** have been given these legs to stand on. One of the legs is God the Father, the other is Jesus. God gives us the strength to stand for that which we **believe** in. Jesus gives us the strength of guidance to know that what we are standing for (what we **believe** in) is Good and true (knowing the difference between

Good and Evil, Right or Wrong). This applies to **EVERYONE** including women and the "sinners" of the Earth. We all have time to change Our ways and follow Jesus, it is never too late. When Jesus comes to **Judge** us then it will be too late. This should be fun not as difficult or impossible as we believe it to be. Take God and Jesus into **EVERY** aspect of your life.

So I must thank God for giving me the knowledge and ability to write this book and must thank Jesus for keeping me guided. If this book was no more than a finger painting I would still have to give thanks to God for giving me the knowledge to perform that alone. I assure you this is much more than a finger painting. So, thank you to God, Jesus, and my parents for helping me persevere through this book and allowing me to (slowly but surely) discover all of their good grace here on Earth. I understand that I am nothing more than an Instrument (Man) for (of) God. Hope you all enjoy. Amen.

Welcome to the Revelation of my Revelation. Thank you Lord. Amen.

Read before you read:

- Considering that Jesus was from the Middle East he was most likely to be brown skinned with characteristics of the common Middle Eastern citizen.
  - o So if he is perceived as "Arab" would that change your perspective on Him?

Enjoy.

Genesis and Original Sin:
The Riddle of Adam and Eve

Before you start reading ask yourself, "When should I tell my kid's about the birds and the bees?"

Have you ever had **thoughts** or **ideas** that you felt like you had no choice but to at least right down? Well if you haven't it is a very interesting and overwhelming experience. If you want to know what it's like; fill up your bath tub, leave the room with the water still on, and let it sit there for a few days. We all know what comes next; flood in the house and a pretty big mess to clean up. Let's just say my brain was the tub, my **thoughts** were the water, and my Life was the house.

This all started May 3rd, 2010 in Fayetteville, Arkansas where I was attending school at the time. I'm from St. Louis Missouri and felt out of place in the new environment. I started to feel reclusive and somewhat distant from the social atmosphere. I always question my-self in times of distress. When I get down about something I torture myself trying to figure out why it happened and how to fix the problem. I've struggled with girls my whole life, having maybe 1 or 2 girlfriends, each only lasting maybe 3 months at most. I'm not aiming for a sob story but this is the catalyst of how this all began.

This dilemma in my adolescent-adult life really pushed me to question my flaws and why I've struggled with girls so much when at the same time I have no trouble making friends. An exception of this came while down in Arkansas, I struggled a lot trying to make friends. Finally, in May during our second semester finals I reached my breaking point. One night I was studying for a final that I had the next day and ended up in the hospital with food poisoning, completely dehydrated and feeling miserable (Thanks Robby, drive through Chinese place not a good idea haha). Stress about my finals, along with the above stated stressors led to my current status. A few days later I slipped into a manic episode (bath tub example) which is a symptom of Bi-Polar disorder (I was diagnosed bi-polar in May 2010 and in January 2011 the diagnosis was changed to a brief psychotic episode, Thank You God). It's ironic that this should happen to me considering my favorite subject is psychology (which I pursued to try and figure out my problems with girls haha). But I will never forget the first thought that sparked the episode. This **thought** altered the very course of my life.

I remember the night vividly. I was watching the Discovery channel show, "Into the Universe with Stephen Hawkings". It was a show about Stephen Hawking's **theories** and **ideas** about the Universe. The part in the show that snagged my attention was his **theory** about how planets and matter are created. He believes that at the far reaches of the Universe there is a force similar to a black hole that creates planets and everything that makes up our Universe. This led me to the thought of the separation of the Science view of our existence vs. the Religious view of our existence. The question I asked myself was, "Why couldn't God be the "original scientist", Could we even go as far as seeing the Universe as part of God's Machinery or the product of God's knowledge and machinery?"

Science is mankind's way of discovering, learning, and explaining God's knowledge. Science is trying to understand and explain the rules that the Earth and Universe governs Us by. The only thing that Science seems to forget or lose sight of is the fact that the Universe is governed by these same similar rules along with a few others. Just like you have to learn about Einstein's or Newton's theories in class; Mankind, along with these same men, are learning and explaining God's theories, works, and ways. So, in a way, God is the Ultimate Scientist/Engineer/Artist/Creator which makes Him the Ultimate Teacher.

It makes sense to think that way because obviously everything has to start and come from some beginning source, at least that's what the Law of **Cause and Effect** tells us. Saint Thomas Aquinas, a theological philosopher, stated, "There must be a first mover existing above all – and this we call God." I couldn't find the actual quote but, Aquinas was also quoted as saying that the combination of scientific reason and spiritual guidance (religion) is needed for Mankind to find peace and the answer's we are seeking here on Earth. Once again, Science itself states that for **Effect** there has to be a **Cause** to create the **Effect**. **I've come to the conclusion that Eve, Earth, and Science are the last 3 "Mysteries" to discover from the Bible to pave the way for God and Jesus' return**.

No matter if you think God is against this notion, I think we all have to agree that they are Real, they are there, and always will be. I think if we calm down and get an understanding of them God will be o.k. with it.

I read an interesting quote in an article, "The Odds Against Life" by George Caylor. Dr. Harold Marowitz, a theoretics expert at Yale University, stated "The odds of life randomly happening is like throwing 4 billion pennies into the air with all of them landing heads-up." Caylor includes in his article another finding of Dr. Marowitz's, "After studying the complexity of a protein molecule, Dr. Morowitz concluded that the probability of life occurring by chance is 1/10236. 1/10236 takes into account all the atoms in the Universe, and the chance that the right ones came together just once to form a protein molecule." The coming together of random protein molecules is obviously **extremely** unlikely to happen by random chance alone; especially considering the sophisticated and complex creatures of life that manifested (resulted) from these protein molecules.

I used these quotes in a project I had in philosophy class. There was a group in the class that was against the thought of God creating Us and the Universe. I asked them the question, "If we are a random creation of the Universe than how come something complex like a computer doesn't appear out of thin air? Why don't we see anything at all randomly appear?" You have to admit that it is a valid argument considering that much **thought** and **knowledge** was put into the making of all our advanced technology today. So how could the complexity and consistency of humans, animals, and systems of Nature be randomly assembled to work perfectly by a mere explosion? Along with this comes the question of how can random molecules come together to work/function, perfectly regulating the systems of our body? Give us **instinct** and **knowledge** to survive, let alone **knowledge** to Create (be Creators like our Father the Original Creator)? Just the functioning of our brain, mind, and body together; regulating itself without impeding the use of our Conscious mind should be evidence enough to make people understand that there has to be a knowledgeable Being that put all of these intangibles together, let alone, make sure they work (have to work perfectly, I might add, or survival for the vessel is impossible).

Outside of nature and its creatures, the Universe has "Laws" imposed on it that every piece of matter, molecule, and atom has no choice but to abide by. Some Examples:

- The Law of Gravity
- The Law of Cause and Effect

- The Law of Conservation of Energy
- Law of Matter and Energy
- Biggest of all- Law of Attraction

Just like society has police to make sure the established "Laws" here are followed, who or what makes sure that the absolute, unchanging "Laws" of the Universe are followed and never defied? Just like a machine, the Universe needs to be monitored and fixed up if any irregularities come up. Let's think about the concept of a Gardner and Herdsman. The garden is beautiful, in order, and looks wonderful if taken care of and monitored. If the Gardner gets lazy and doesn't take care of the garden it will lose its beauty and order, becoming a place of chaos and disorder. If the Herdsman doesn't watch over and keep order of his flock, the Sheppard will lose control of the Herd and will only be able to stand by and watch the Herd disperse. When your computer breaks down do you just let it sit there and fix itself? No, there is a more knowledgeable person to fix your computer for you.

Right there we should see that outside help is a **NECESSITY** in every aspect of our life. Of course there's the exception of the **Beginning/ Original Creation** of matter, Earth, all of the species there in, and the very Universe itself. I don't understand how or why we can't all come to the agreement that somehow, someway [(ways Mankind is slowly starting to understand (key word there "slowly")] the Universe had to be "**Created**". Go back to the random computer question I asked the class. Building it took time, thought, good ideas, shitty ideas, failures, advances, work, **tools**, and **help** to build. Yes, you heard me correct. I said **TOOLS** and **HELP**. Think about all of the angels that were/are in Heaven. You think God just let them sit around while he builds the **ENTIRE F****** UNIVERSE**? No. Doesn't making a child take a man (God) and a woman (Earth), keep readin' ladies I got ya. This doesn't take credit away from God at all. From Genesis we are taught that we are made in God's "**Image**", what he pictured, planned, the layout, the blueprint he put together to build Us. You don't think God had a Plan or Image for the Universe? **Genesis just gives Mankind a simple overview of his Plan**. Yet, it is blatantly obvious what Genesis is and stands for.

I will admit that I think Genesis is a stretch and kind of farfetched, **IT'S A RIDDLE**. Hold on, let's think about Genesis. No matter your beliefs about God or the beginning of Creation of the Universe, picture yourself as a parent. When your 4 or 5 year old hears about a newborn baby and innocently walks over to you, looks up at you holding his stuffed animal and asks, "Dad where do babies come from?" Do you say, "Well son, what happens is that I get my "man part" real hard and put it into your mommy's "girl part", and that's how it's done son? Haha hell no. I hope you don't. We tell them a bird or stork comes to the house and drops them off. We don't explain the complexities of **Creation (birth) here on Earth** to them until they are older and have developed the body parts, knowledge, and emotions necessary (needed) to perform the act of sex (**Creation**). **GENESIS AND THE STORY OF THE STORK= THE ORIGINAL PARABLE**. God saved the birds and bees story of Creating the Universe for the teenage-adolescent years (**Now**). Just like a 4 or 5 year old is not mature and developed enough to learn about sex; Mankind had not yet developed/attained the knowledge necessary to understand the way that God created the Universe (**Parallel**). That's why I think Genesis looks like a lullaby or a kid's story Dad reads right before bed. Genesis is Mankind's original Dr. Seuss story. We were just babies then, so God kept Genesis short and simple.

Actually, sex should be the main defense for God and His existence. **Sex is the answer to the mystery behind Genesis and Earth**. Animals and Humans aren't "ready" or "able" to have sex for years (animal kingdom depends on the species; humans aren't till at least 13 or 14). Getting to the ability to have sex takes time and development of the mind and body. The first Months-Years of our life involve no sexual thought or realization. Think about it. What do babies love to do and hate to wear? Rip off and not wear clothes. Babies could care less if they are naked or clothed, no matter who or how many people are around. In fact, if I'm correct, it's always a battle to dress or diaper babies. Am I right? Sound a little familiar? Haha this is the story of **Adam and Eve**, the Beginning, the **Babies of Mankind**. Lucifer probably came by and told Eve she was puttin' on some weight haha, and so of course she thinks Adam thinks she's fat and puts some clothes on. So because his girl put clothes on Adam had no choice but to follow suit to keep her happy. Just like growing up (sexual development), we see that no longer can we stay naked and keep playing in the Garden of Eden (be a child). This also makes a lot of sense considering that for the first 5-6 years of a child's life we are in the "**Imagination Stage**", where children think they have imaginary friends, play superhero, just being kid's having fun in whatever they do. Every adult sees how happy kids are and envy that. In the movie "Knocked Up" Seth Rogen and Paul Rudd are watching Paul Rudd's kid's play around in the park. They are playing with bubbles or something simple but, are happier than either Seth or Paul can remember being. Seth says to Paul, "I wish I enjoyed anything as much as that."

We individually "**Fall from Eden**" once our "**Imagination Stage**" ends, when we realize we can't be children anymore. We see we have to wear clothes. Taught throughout the whole "**Imagination Stage**" that we "Can be whatever we want to be." That soon turns to "You have to go to school and work!" Which directs our paths and lives according to this so called **Reality**; we all say the same thing, "Time to face reality and give up on the dreams". That's where tuning into your **iGod** (learning to use (pray) and listen (opening eyes and ears) to our shrouded and buried **Soul**) will give you the ability to start your climb back up to Eden, it begins in your mind.

All of this makes sense considering that girls "mature" at a faster rate than boys do (First one to "**Bite the Apple**"). Girls become sensitive and develop more insecurities at a faster rate than boys do. Girls feel the "**Effect**" of **Original Sin** at a younger age because they bit the apple first. Considering how annoyingly sensitive Girls are this all makes sense. Here are the statistics of Eating Disorders in America:

- 8 Million total cases
- 7 Million- Women
- 1 Million- Men

It's appropriate to use Eating Disorders since eating an apple created your sensitivity levels. But hey at least we know apples are the cause of Eating Disorders haha.

I think my favorite stand-up is Daniel Tosh's "Totally Serious". He actually talks about the Adam and Eve dilemma. He talks about how Eve ate the apple and women's resulting punishment (=) painful child-birth and menstrual cycles or whatever. Then he says, "Man's punishment. Dealing with women." Haha. This isn't my point, though very funny. He then switches to the topic of how everyone thinks "God hates queers", and says, "God doesn't hate queers he's just pissed that they found a loop-hole in his system." Alright ladies and "queers", I'm not trying to poke fun at either of you. Actually quite the opposite; this book is meant to help you, Science, and more importantly our Mom, Earth or "Mother Nature" (God's wife, Our Mom).

So this thought of needing time to develop an understanding for the art of Creation here on Earth (sex) is then mirrored with the mystery of why Genesis is so farfetched like a lullaby to a baby. Like I mentioned before, **"The Father of Modern Science"** Isaac Newton, didn't discovery gravity or the basics of Science until 1666 years after Jesus was here which is even thousands more years after Genesis was written. So why would God break out the physics and calculus books in Genesis when the most sophisticated piece of technology was maybe a pulley system? This would be like trying to teach a 3 year old physics. To further explain the earlier explanation with the Dr. Seuss books, I believe that mankind's advancement over time can be paralleled with the development of a child. If we look back at the past and see where our knowledge and technology began, compared to now, we see that slowly but surely Mankind began to advance our knowledge and technology to where we are today. Just like a kid growing up, going through school. They start at the very simple basics: Reading, spelling, basic math. Then gradually move on to progressively harder subjects like: biology, calculus, chemistry, and so on… When mankind first recognized Science we didn't start building iPods, we didn't even know what the hell a wheel was. When we start pre-school we aren't expected to pass the A.C.T, we don't even know the difference between the letters A, C, and T. Just like if a little boy and little girl are playing together, they aren't thinking about having sex, they barely know the difference between the female sex and the male sex. That should clear up confusion on why God didn't give us the details on His knowledge and machinery in Genesis.

To piece the puzzle of Religion and Science with a better more concrete example, we must go back to the concept of **Cause** and **Effect** again. Thinking about **Creating a Child**, the Creation of the Universe also needs a Man (God) and Woman (Science). Once again, we know Genesis is the **"Idea"** or **"plan"** (the **"Cause"** behind the creation of the Universe) of the

Universe while Science is/are the **TOOLS/HELP**, we discussed earlier, used to actually **Create/ Build** the Universe **[(the tools/help (Science) used and product (the Universe) are the "Effect (s)" that follows the original "Cause" (Genesis)]**. Because thinking of the conception of a child, the man's semen or genetics (the idea of the child) passes into the woman, who has to go through pregnancy (the tools used to create the child) which **both combine to Create** the child; because, one without the other cannot conceive a child. God is not exempt from this either, and don't worry he's not ashamed of it and has been waiting for us to figure this out. Since the Earth is our Mom we have to go back to the conception of a child. God designed Mankind from his "Man part" haha. "Putting" his "genetics" on (or "in") Earth with everything we need to survive. The reason the Earth is our Mom is because while on Earth we are in Mother Nature's (Mom's) Womb. The thing that is being developed or "conceived", you could say, is our **Soul** (**iGod**). We all go through a Second birth (Rebirth) after we die, when we enter eternal life. So when we die we are going through birth again, reborn in the presence of our Dad in Heaven. This explains why God isn't present on Earth with us yet. During the 9 months of development in the Womb we are only a-part of our Mom, only "knowing" we came from and have Dad's genetics.

It just feels weird to talk about which also makes sense. We would all throw up if we talked to our parents about their sexual activities. So now it's time to grow up, mature and bring Mom and Dad back together who split because of Us in the first place. "Was it my fault Mommy that Dad left?" Yes, it is Our fault Mankind. And too correct the problem we have to bring **ALL** of the **FAMILY** (the whole World) back together and have a big family meeting (or party as I like to think). Those who don't want to discover Our Dad through Jesus will be kept from the party. These are the keys God has been waiting for his Kid's/Mankind to figure out:

- Understand the Adam and Eve dilemma.
- Give Moms and Science the credit and respect they deserve in the Creation of Us and the Universe. We don't lose respect or Fear of the Father (God). We just come to an agreement that it makes sense that God would use the Knowledge of Science to make Us and the Universe. Just like we can all agree that Women are needed to create our kids.
- The Earth (Living body, later chapter) is literally the body of our Mom, "Mother Nature".

Parallels/Parables

First, let's remember that in the Bible and Theologians will agree that God is described as a Being of **Omniscient** (**infinite knowledge**). Just like Scientists will agree that energy has always been ("can't be created or destroyed"). The first thing I realized that connected all of this is the fact that we live in a Parallel Universe. Everything is parallel in this world:

- Earth and Hell.
- Earth and Purgatory.
- Men and Women.
- Science and Religion.
- Republicans and Democrats.
- Most the Religions around the World.

I think Science expected Genesis to be an instruction manual on how God created everything (tell us about "**sex**"). If the Bible were written today it probably would have since Mankind is "older" and has the knowledge to understand how God made the Universe. Think about it, just like **teaching** about sex, parents don't read their **kids** Ernest Hemingway, they read them Dr. Seuss. When I see the word Genesis I think that it looks very similar to Genius (Parallel- Genesis=Genius). All though Genesis means the beginning or creation; I think that it also refers to "God's Genius".

Once again, Genesis, to me, seems to be a simple overview for Us on how God created the Universe. Also, Jesus never mentioned anything about Science or how God created Everything. Once again, if we think back to the time that Jesus was around and how he taught his followers it's pretty easy to see why Jesus never brought anything up about "Science". Jesus' teachings were very simplistic comparing God's word with examples from nature or of common people (parables=parallels). Jesus made his lessons very simple and understandable for the people of the time who don't seem too bright, we can agree they aren't nearly as smart as we are today.

Along with defining and discovering our Modern Science Isaac Newton spent most of his time trying to decipher the Bible and the **mysteries/ riddles** God left us to find. I found this out from a show on the History Channel called "The Nostradamus Effect". The show is about all of the predictions of the end of the world. The show talked about how Newton would spend nearly 18 hours a day (!!!) going through the Bible and trying to figure these riddles out (and I thought I was crazy for thinking about it so much). Also, ironically, Newton discovered his "Law of Gravity" in 1666 (Kind of eerie). I think it is also ironic that he discovered gravity from an apple falling from a tree. It mirrors what happened in Eden with Adam and Eve. Maybe the apple wasn't the "knowledge of good and evil" it's probably the knowledge or awareness of the laws (Science) imposed on Us and the Universe. I just think that God knew that if man possessed the "knowledge of good and evil" some would dedicate themselves to follow and understand Him, while some would follow and understand his laws (Science), each separating from the other (creating the parallel between each). One would fall in Love and totally dedicate themselves to the Father (God) while the others would fall in Love and totally dedicate themselves to the Mother (Science). We also have to agree that much evil has been done in their names (In "Religions" name and "Science'" name). So when considering God and science just remember the Law of **Cause** and **Effect**. And consider the question, as of right now; could we be trying to pair Religion with the wrong study of Science?

Lastly, Science has somehow (I don't know how you could even come close to a hypothesis like this) come to the conclusion that the Universe is growing and expanding outwards. O.k. I'll buy it, but let me ask you this, what the hell is it expanding towards or growing in? Once again this scientific claim supports God. Obviously, God created the Universe. We don't know where, how, or what God used to make It. I see whatever the Universe is expanding into or contained in as something like an observatory in God's laboratory (Heaven). It makes sense. God has put us into a finite "space" to keep an eye on (observe) and take care of. In Genesis God states, "I give man control of all the beasts on the land and sea." So, whatever our Universe and World is contained in could be compared to a Zoo. Let me explain. Zoos are where we contain animals (in a finite "space"), to take care of and keep an eye on (observe). This is a perfect comparison. We go to a Zoo to watch (observe) the exotic animals in it. Seeing the animals interact in the pseudo-environment is entertaining, bringing joy and amazement to the observer. The Bible teaches us that Mankind is God's most prized creation, and is always watching over us. I'm sure that God finds joy and amazement in watching us interact in our finite, pseudo-environment (Earth). I don't know about you but I can't wait to leave this finite World and enter our true environment (Heaven), don't worry I'm not suicidal or hate life I just can see the boundless potential and possibilities with God in Heaven. Cage any animal what will they do if given the chance? **Escape**. Our **Soul** is the caged "**Spirit**" in us all, let it out.

Also, it seems that everyone has forgotten to take into account the existence of Dinosaurs. If the creation of the Universe was a random, onetime occurrence, humanity would've existed with Dinosaurs and would've been wiped out along with the Dinosaurs. I highly Doubt that humanity would've made it through the blast (considering reptiles and sea animals were the only survivors after the blast). Unless Science has pulled the shades over our eyes making up Dinosaurs to be a fairy tale for simplistic people of the world (Us) to believe; merely an attempt to give their argument some back bone... I don't see it like this because we are led to believe that Dinosaurs are the source that oil comes from. This proves God's existence in itself; because of the fact that a **purpose** and **use** manifested out of their death for Mankind [(=) oil]. This means that the creation and extinction of the Dinosaurs **had** to be a part of a **bigger plan** or "**The Plan**". And think about that, if Dinosaurs wouldn't have existed and there was no oil for man to base their technology on, where would our advanced civilizations be today? What would transportation be like? How would everything be powered? O yea, I apologize, I forgot that Dinosaurs' sacrifice for Mankind's benefit to better our technology and studies, was just a stroke of luck by a fucking explosion, just a flip of the coin that luckily landed heads up for mankind. Well since it was just a stroke of luck and random chance, there's no one to thank for creating and making sure the unimaginable, impossibly complex Laws, forces, and matter of the Universe came together to function **perfectly** on a continuous, unchanging, consistent basis. I guess we can just give a sigh of relief and wipe our brow for the fact that it worked out in our favor. Bull Shit! Are you kidding me?

Since we can infer that humanity wasn't here before the extinction of Dinosaurs, how did humanity get here other than by Divine intervention (God putting us here)? Was there another "Not so Big Bang"? Or did we just find the best hiding places on the planet when the Asteroid hit? People don't give enough thought (if any at all) to the complex make up of the Universe or to the carefully thought out **plan** God had/has for the Universe and Us.

Here's where **Cause** and **Effect** come into play. I sum this up with an example of mine. I see the differences between Science and Religion in a simple act such as turning on a television from a distance. I look at the existence of the Universe and Us as the television being turned on by a remote. I see the religious view as just thinking that the T.V. turns on by the person (God) without the use of the remote, not considering that the person (God) **had to use/do something** to turn on the T.V. I see the science belief as just believing the remote (Science) can turn on the T.V. without an outside force (God), and never consider that the button of the remote **had/has** to be pushed by someone to turn the T.V. on; because, without the person (God) to push the button on the remote (Science) the T.V. cannot and will not be turned on. Religion never thinks about how God Caused (tools used, or "words spoken") the Universe and Us to come into existence and are jealous/scared that Science is starting to explain this/ these tools (**Effect's**). So, combining the 2 views into 1 shows that with the combination of God pushing the button on the remote, the T.V. will turn on. This will explain both **Cause** and **Effect**. Basically, saying that if you're sitting on the couch with a remote, the person on the couch can't turn on the T.V. without the remote; **paralleled** with the remote cannot turn on the T.V. without the person (God). Going back to the law of **Cause** and **Effect**, Religion can only explain the **Cause** (God) never thinking of what he did to Create everything, while Science can only explain the **Effect** (the small amount of what we have seen in the Universe and the Laws that govern **Earth, the Universe, and everything in it**; of which have no choice but to abide by).

So why does science and religion have to be separate? If God is so opposed to science why hasn't he put a stop to it? I do believe that eventually we will create our own destruction with technology leading to Revelations. But either way if you see technology in this sense as obviously seeming evil, you have to take into account the benefits our technology has provided for health and our society. Today our lives **rely** on technology. Also, if technology will lead to our destruction, it is a necessary evil in God's eyes because it's a-part of his **plan** to lead to Revelations.

I think there are a few things that Science finds hard to believe in the existence of God (the feud about the beginning of the Universe being the main dilemma between the 2). Secondly, people expect there to be an insanely difficult scientific formula to prove or disprove God's existence. Going back to combining the 2 perspectives of Science and Religion, wouldn't combining 2 different fields of study, to discover an answer seem pretty difficult in itself? Combining spiritual guidance (mysteries of the Bible and God), positive (+) energy or knowledge, with Empirical reasoning (Science), another positive (+) energy or knowledge, seems like it is more difficult than any equation that Science itself could muster up.

- Can We (Mankind) challenge ourselves to beat our false belief about **only** opposites attracting [(positive (+) attracts negative (-)] our current world abides by? And change our belief to follow the Universal Law of Attraction which says Like attracts Like [positive (+) attracting positive (+) | and negative (-) attracting negative (-)].

I think we can do it and beat this perceived impossibility. Honestly, I believe that if we want to discover God we must combine both of these theories and ideas, open both (2) eyes instead of just searching with 1.

Lastly, I see Jesus as the last obstacle that Science sees with God. I believe that it goes beyond the seemingly "impossible" miracles that he performed and goes back to our basic human nature. People look at Jesus and his connection with God and ask the question, "why is he so special? And why doesn't God talk to me or others?" So in a sense I think that people see themselves as very self-important, jealous of the fact that Jesus had a direct line to God and Heaven while we can't and won't until He returns. Humble yourself, you're not Jesus, **only a man**.

This thought of Science and God sparked the fire of my manic episode. A manic episode is having uncontrollable, racing thoughts. You could say my thoughts were racing but that is a complete understatement. My mind started to think and connect things without control. Some of what I was thinking was delusional, but some of them (I think) are pretty creative and thought provoking, they are the ones this book is about.

The Parallels of our Parallel Universe are what this book is about. I've only found a few but the ones I have found seem pretty real. Just a reminder, in the New Testament Jesus' teaching's were referred to as **Parables**, which are **Parallels**. Jesus always explained his lessons with things of nature or common people (Parallels between God's Word and Nature). I also believe that Jesus himself was paralleled with a part of nature, but I will discuss that later.

Lastly, here's something I wonder about:

- If mankind/life is just a random phenomenon of the Universe, with no importance to it, this would mean that our (and any other life form, if any exist) existence could be wiped out at anytime with no effect on the Universe itself. So, would the Universe truly exist with no one there to witness it?

Parallels of Science and Religion: Rectifying Original Sin.

A pair of parallel lines will continue forward never touching for an infinite amount of time. Almost like a race if you will, to an end neither will ever reach alone. Both are heading in the same direction to the end goal just on 2 distinctly different paths. The lines are kept separate by the opposing charges each possesses. Just like 2 magnets repelling from each other. If both paths were altered leading them to meet in the middle combining forces continuing to that same, before stated, destination, could it be possible for the 2 lines to meet their end goal faster and more efficiently? The end goal (=) Explaining the Universe and Our existence; reaching an answer (=) a positive (+) outcome (Happiness).

These 2 make up the **Atom** of the Universe. One of them is the **Proton** (+) and one is the **Electron** (-), both of them circling the **Nucleus**, or the end goal each is trying to reach by themselves. Both are trying to explain the same thing (reaching the answer to God and our Creator), but are **Parallel**; each explaining it in entirely different ways; both having holes in their argument that the other can fill, **Opposing Forces** (different theories). We can all agree that religion and science have opposite charges (different ideas), one with a positive (+) charge and one with a negative (-) charge. False. I will agree that they see the end goal differently; but regardless if they see the same thing differently, they are still looking at and trying to figure out **THE SAME EXACT THING**, getting to the **Nucleus** (God). We can all agree that they are parallel and oppose each other. If continued on this path, this feud would wage on forever neither one finding the answer, with the end goal staying **Neutral**, never attaining that positive (+) outcome of an answer no matter what it is. There will be no positive (+) "happy" outcome. At least, we can agree that they **think** they are opposites and continue to prove this in accordance with **The Law of Attraction**. It's time to correct the **thought** that only opposites [positive (+) and negative (-) energy] attract.

I believe that truly Religion and Science are attracted to each other; it's just people **think** it's impossible for them to touch or come together. Yes, Religion and Science seem like opposing forces, one positive (+) and the other negative (-). But, because Our World is run by men who act like 3 year olds, each force believes they are the positive (+) and the other is the negative (-) charge; scared of the **thought** that if they are the negative (-) charge they will die (I guess I have no idea haha). Science's theory of metal's attraction (magnets) has created this false belief leading us to **think** that this is true and only opposites attract. So technically, by this definition alone shouldn't these 2 have already combined together?

Opposites do attract but they both see the positive (+) and **neutral** outcome (meeting in the middle to accomplish something, the **Nucleus**). With magnets, positive (+) attracts and links to negative (-). Their end goal is to combine and link together; which, magnets will do without hesitation when given the chance. Once again, we must go back to men and women. Obviously, polar opposites; yet, they come together to **Create** a positive (+) outcome, a child, that each had to meet in the middle (a **Neutral** end goal) to make. They reached the **Nucleus** because **they worked together**. Just because they are opposites, doesn't make one better than the other or one good one evil; each contains equal amounts of positive (+) energy that **HAS** to be combined and utilized to reach the **Nucleus** (the child).

If we think about it the Earth is a magnet (North and South Pole). Throughout history we see Mankind, as a whole, is a magnet. We are driven by and entertained by the **thought** of opposing forces clashing:

1. War.
2. Racism (Black or White).
3. All the different Religions.
4. Men and Women.
5. The plots in all movies and books is between the hero [Protagonist (+)] vs. the villain [Antagonist (-)]. Actually, if we think about it, either Evil is defeated or the characters come to a mutual agreement (sometimes becoming friends).
6. Politics (Republicans vs. Democrats).
7. And obviously our fascination with athletics (Don't get me wrong I have a very competitive spirit and love to play sports but, from an early age kids are taught that life is a competition. One team vs. the other... pick a side kid and stick with it) the clashing of opposing forces (Offense and Defense) trying to get the same end goal (Win). But each team must have a Succesful Offense and Defense. Each important facet of the team is distinctly opposite from the other but both must be equally strong for the team to be successful and win.

All of the above stated examples have the same end goal; be better than and conquer the other. Everyone wants the world to change and be a better place but no one wants to make a move and redefine the lines of reality that have been railed into are brain ("Mind F*****" As P. Diddy said in "Get Him to the Greek"). We all talk about "changing the world"; but, once again we all forget about the main word in that statement, **Change**. Not trying to rant, just telling people to grow up and see that the things we **think** are repelling each other are truly attracting each other, needing the other to survive and reach the goal they are failing to reach alone, which is the case for Religion and Science.

Religions today live by the thought of positive (+) and negative (-) energy. You are either good (+) or evil (-), Heaven (+) or Hell (-). This split is only creating **judgment** (the **Original Sin**). God, Jesus, and the Bible teach us that **judgment** is wrong and **not our concern**. Yet, everyone condemns the other based on what they **think** God would **think** about that person. Think about a family; parents with 2 kids for example. Each sibling aggravates and angers the other. We've all heard of "telling on" someone. All the way through childhood each sibling will do this to the other out of their understandable childish nature. If a report is serious enough, it is understandably necessary that the sibling would tell on the other. But, if they continually tell on the other sibling or give their opinion to the parents about what they believe to be the necessary punishment, the parent or parents will become furious from frustration (especially considering these reports of misbehaving are more than likely simplistic, annoying). It's not the child's concern whether to discipline the other sibling or condemn him to the type of punishment given (left to the parents to decide, not the **children**). Just like we are all God's children, each of us condemns the other trying to make ourselves feel better (we are the good one) out of the other's despair. **Judgment** is not our concern. And this **Curse of Judgment** that has befallen Mankind is… **The Original Sin (=) Doubt of God's existence and his ways/tools used**.

Has anyone ever tried to think about what **Original Sin** truly is? Or how we can fix it and apologize to God? Especially considering it's called the "**Fall of Mankind**", not, "The Fall of Adam and Eve". I think since Adam (Man) and Eve (Women) screwed up, Mankind has been in timeout in our room (Earth) until we realize and rectify what put us here in the first place (**Original Sin**). **We have to** understand that the stigma between Religion and Science is incorrect. God is trying to show us that **Like** should attract **Like**, and **opposites attract to work together and reach a common (Neutral) goal (Nucleus)**. Once again, **Like** attracted to **Like** is the **Law of Attraction**.

We all can't deny that Religion and the Laws of Science equally exist. Don't you think God would find it pretty cool to combine the theories of Religion with Science to further discover **HIS Universe**?

Anyway here are some examples of the **Law of Attraction**: the rich get richer the poor get poorer. Americans think about terrorism which just creates more terrorism. The only thing that is talked about with the economy is that it is terrible, which just leads to more debt and worse unemployment. Beefing up the war on drugs doesn't stop drugs, it only leads to more drug users and further debt from wasted time and man power on simple recreation drugs like marijuana for example. The list goes on, I could write a whole book just on examples of the **Law of Attraction** in the World right now, I bet you could too.

An easier way to think about the **Law of Attraction** is think of it is a fuel source. If you dream to be rich and abundant and you focus all of your Being to accomplish that goal because you believe that it will bring you happiness than you can and with the right mentality you will. The **Law of Attraction** says that the power is in **thought** and your feelings about that thought. If you feel strongly about earning that money and devise a plan to do that you probably will. But when your **Pursuit of Happiness** is for such a big, finite goal alone; you will only find happiness in pursuing that one goal and will not be able to find happiness until that goal is accomplished. Once you finally feel like you have accomplished your goal, through selfish human nature you will need more "**Fuel**" to keep that fire of happiness burning in you. And once again that happiness will only come from earning more money. This example of money is obviously greed. I'm not saying that it is bad to set your sights on getting some money in life but don't tell yourself that that is the only thing that will make you happy, because money can only make the fire burn inside you for so long.

I use Jesus as my example of how to "**Fuel up**". Once you get to the place of gratitude, being thankful for everything you have; being thankful for the very ability to breath and think, everything that happens to you becomes a source of happiness. The "Bad-times" you're going through won't seem so bad. The way that Jesus gained positive (+) energy or gained happiness was by pleasing others and making others happy. He didn't gain happiness from people praising him, he was so happy and powerful because he knew he was helping people and was making a difference. We all can, I'll further explain this in the chapter about praying and using your **iGod** (your **Soul**).

God wants the **Law of Attraction** to be applied to the whole world which would lead to the attraction of positive (+) to positive (+). Going back to what we talked about before about Religion and Science being stubborn, both wanting to be the positive (+) charge and condemn the other to be the negative (-) charge. Both believe themselves to be positive (+) and the other negative (-), each having applicable, valid theories and explanations (good enough to make them emulate positive (+) energy/knowledge) that **Parallel** each other. We think that opposites attract, well if we think about what was just said we see that they are not opposites at all but are actually following the **Law of Attraction**.

Each having good/valid reasons to be positive (+) about in their theories will attract people to either one of the establishments giving that establishment more positive (+) energy. But, when confronted by each other, each side gets insecure, becoming defensive against the opposing establishment. While they are getting angry and defensive that positive (+) energy transforms into negative (-) energy creating the tension and bitching we all see between the 2. So, positive (+) force is being used to attract followers, and when each establishment is confronted by the other, that positive (+) switches to negative (-), creating the negative stigma (**have to be separate, cannot work together**) that we know today. So, we can see Religion and Science **have the possibility** to combine their positive (+) forces and attract each other. If they could recognize the positive (+) energy they themselves possess; they then **could** open their selfish, insecure, childish eyes to see the other also possesses equal (=) positive (+) energy. If only they/we could **grow up**, step back and let the **Law of Attraction** work, letting **Like** attract **Like** (Religion and Science attracting one another), we could maybe reach the end goal of Finding God and discovering the rest of our Universe.

Are they not being attracted to the same **Nucleus**, explaining God's existence and the Universe?

- **Proton**= Religion.
- **Electron**= Science.
- **Nucleus**= God or the beginning (explanation) of the Universe.
- **Proton** (+) **Electron** (+) **Nucleus** [positive (+), and **neutral**]= **The Atom** (answer, end goal to the Universe).

So you probably want to scream at me and say, "You really expect people to compromise on something like this? It can't/will not happen because_____… _____." Yep, yep keep filling in the blank. The world will definitely change and get better with that strategy. Obviously this is working. Hahaaha. Uuuummm, no it's not sorry to kill your buzz, but this new strategy is how we begin to pave the way for Jesus and God's return (gain new knowledge). We have to show God that we are sorry for Our (Mankind's) **Original Sin**, and have truly changed our ways. Guess what? We actually have to **grow up** and be **mature**, work together, coexist, open our eyes to see 1World not 100 nations, maybe look at it with a positive attitude and have fun with it knowing that working together we are going to discover so much more, maybe act like the adults we think we are and not be so **Egotistic**. We believe that our Egotistic tendency's disappear after childhood but our **Ego** is where **Original Sin** and the **Virus of Judgment Lives** (where Lucifer resides here on Earth).

Baptism at birth does not at all rid us of **Original Sin**. You have to have a personal relationship with God first to **try** and rid yourself of it, become a positive (+) force for God. Everyone on the planet is on their own "**Spiritual Journey**" that goes beyond just finding God; your "**Journey**" is to discover who **YOU** truly are, the type of **Spirit** you are whether it is a **Holy Spirit** or not. We are all **Neutral energy**, containing **Potential Energy**, circling around a very powerful, untapped, unlimited central force of energy, the "**Nucleus**" of the Universe, if you will. We are all held circling or revolving around the **Nucleus** (personally I see the **Nucleus** as **God/Jesus**, but as we all know this is open to interpretation) by the same force that the Earth is held to the Sun by, **Gravity**. Most people call this the previously stated, "**Spiritual Journey**". This "**Journey**", like planets in the Universe, is governed and kept in revolution around the **Nucleus** by "**Spiritual Gravity**". Our **Soul** (your **iGod**) is the part of us that contains our **Potential Energy** and is controlled/governed by the **Nucleus** and its "**Spiritual Gravity**". Once again, all of our **Souls** can be seen combining and making up this **Atom**. In this case a very very very large **Atom** that has every **Soul** (**iGod**) revolving around it no matter what they believe in.

Free-Will and the Conscious mind are the results of the **Original Sin**. Our Conscious Mind and Free-Will dictates what type of **Kinetic Energy** (**Proton** or **Electron**) our dormant (**Neutral**), **Potential Energy** contained in our **Soul** (**iGod**) will transform to. **The knowledge of Good and Evil** is Mankind's awareness (Free-Will) of the potential/ability to use our knowledge as a Good, happy (**Proton**) source of positive (+) energy; or Evil, unhappy/miserable (**Electron**), negative (-) source/force of **Energy**. Honestly, we should see our **Journey** as a video game:

- A good example is the game **Fable**. In the game you can choose to be Good or Bad. Your character slowly earns experience points giving him stronger powers for his equipment or whatever. He gets the experience points from situations or opportunities your character encounters in the game. Each situation gives you the option to perform a Good or a Bad act; strengthening your character's Good or Bad energy, making the character a stronger source of Good or Bad energy (stronger **Proton** or stronger **Electron**).

Maybe life's not a video game but it is a story or a movie. We are all characters in the story of Life/Earth whether we want to be the Protagonist (**Proton**) or Antagonist (**Electron**). **It's up to You**. **You choose** the importance of and type of character you're going to play, either strengthening God's part of the story (**Proton**) or Satan's (**Electron**). Now when I say life is like a video game, think that every day you are trying to become a "stronger **Proton**". My definition of being a **Proton** is just being happy. Happiness is what will make your Soul (**iGod**) stronger; happiness is your "Fuel". Either way, our Free-Will chooses and the resulting choices define our part (Protagonist or Antagonist) in the story of Earth/Life. We can all agree that choosing to be good or bad has been an obvious decision to make since the beginning of time. And we can agree the **Original Sin/Judgment** results from picking 1 side or the other, nothing in between. Maybe, we need to choose to be like the **Nucleus** (Jesus).

Now pump your brakes and here me out. **This is exactly what God wants us to do** and is the reason he sent Jesus to Earth; to show us to be 2 in 1 [**Proton** (God/Father) and **Neutron** (Jesus/Son)]. Once again, we are all God's children (including Jesus who is our older brother who deserves a sign of respect for saving our ass/existence; at least a thank you for what he did and went through). That means, being the **children we still are**, we look to Dad to **learn** how to do things and to get an idea of how to live our life. Because, we all want to be like our Dad; I don't know about you but I know I look up to and want to be like my Dad (my example of how to be a man). Likewise, with God, we all want to be like Him whether we'll admit it or not. You'd be crazy and I will tell you to your face, you're a terrible liar if you don't envy the **power and knowledge** our Father possesses; that would go against Mankind's **Egotistic** childish nature. Becoming like our Dad (God) has always been a possibility and always will be.

If you're wondering if I think people have succeeded at becoming like God, **Yes**, some have succeeded successfully in God's eyes as a **Proton** (Nelson Mandela, Mother Theresa, Martin Luther King, the list goes on but you get the idea). Along with being a strong **Proton** (attracting positive (+) energy (happiness) from God and their followers, using it as their power source for good) they also were **Neutral** (**Neutron**, just like Jesus) people who knew their mission and were not fazed by outside negative (-) forces. They were very humble people who didn't exploit their power for their own selfish desires, they used their positive (+) energy for God and others, they were great examples of being a "**Nucleus**" **for God**. **True Men and Women of God**. History has shown us that it is possible to be a **strong**

force of good in the world. We've seen what happened to these "Good" people with all of the tribulations they went through and are afraid if we are "Good for God", the same thing will happen to us, and that doesn't seem to fun. No one remembers that being a strong source of good doesn't make you weak, it just seems that way because we **All** (once again) have the false stigma and image that "**Good**" people are a bunch of pussies and won't be "**successful**" and don't have fun in the World. But actually, quite the contrary, these people were by far the strongest most powerful people on the planet including Jesus. They didn't back down from the mission God gave them because of the outside negative (-) force. They stayed on the path and fought till the end, I don't see a whole lot of those people anymore. And guess what, the ways they did everything was the only "Fun" they knew how to have.

Because of this image and God forsaken fear of being "**unsuccessful**" most just harden their heart against God and the World because hey, the whole World's against you, right? Since there is so much evil in the World it seems like the **Electrons** are more powerful, which as of right now they are. History has shown us that these **Electrons** can become very very powerful (Hitler, Napoleon, Sudaam Hussein, Kim Jong il, Iran's leader, Cuba's leader, etc…). They understand how to keep gaining more power and energy. With all of the Fear that is instilled in these nations, the people act as a generator just making them more and more powerful. This is why Dictatorship can't exist. The lust and temptation of the possible power right in front of them is too great to pass up. Eventually they need more and more. So they instill more and more fear, only generating more negative (-) energy for them to use.

What I would like to say to these poor nations. The Dictator's Power Source is in the people, soldiers, and officer he governs. Do not forget he is nothing but a Man. He is only as powerful as you make

him to be. The **Power of Good and Change is in the Masses**. Turn your energy from being the source of the **Electron** and become the **Proton**. God will come and save you once the pull of Positive (+) energy is greater than the negative (-) energy. Because **Like** attracts **Like**, so become the **Proton**, send your fears and prayers to God, he will hear them, feel them and **he will come**; then kick back and watch Satan and his **Electrons** be repelled away. **Be Patient** and know (Believe) you have the **Potential Energy** to do it, look for him and **Be Patient**. So it is time to change that Bull Shit and bring Fear and Power back to God and to the Righteous Men and Women of the World (The **Protons** and **Nucleus'**). Anyone can become a Nucleus for God, I don't care who or what tells you you can't. I want you right now to say to yourself, "Fuck that, I'm ready God." And **He will begin your Journey**. Be patient, pray, and open your eyes and ears to God. You will find Him and He will find You, meet in the middle you could say (**Neutral** task for both of you).

To become the positive (+) force (**Proton**) we try to become like the Dad we see in the **Old Testament**, seemingly very bitter and **Judgmental** towards everyone. I'll admit this is the image we all have of God from the **Old Testament**. Sorry pops, with all due respect. I don't think God knew that he left a window open for error in Mankind. This window of error that back fired on him was Free-Will. Lucifer's plan of revenge (or why ever the Hell he would be pissed/jealous at/of God in paradise) worked by exploiting God's mistake (Free-Will) creating the **Original Sin**. If Lucifer was getting kicked out of Eden (Heaven) he was dragging Mankind down to Hell with Him.

Anyway, Dad had to correct or show people how to use Free-Will the right way unlike our Dumbass brother Lucifer (definitely the black-sheep of the family haha. I bet he's just pissed he's got a chick's name. "Hey there **Lucy!!!**" hahahah… See it's that easy, look at Satan as our older dumbass brother with a gay ass name and he has no more power than anyone of Us. Make him your driving force to attract the Positive (+) energy and repel Negative (-) energy.)

All of our Fear's and Doubt's (sickness, money, war, fear of change, **especially mental abnormalities**...etc) here on Earth only exist with power because of the **Original Doubt Lucy Created**, their awareness and power thrives and survives because we allow them too. To fix the error of Free-Will is where Jesus comes into play (Thank God, Amen).

Back to being like God and a **Proton**. Here is how I back up my claim of God and Jesus making up the **Nucleus** of the Universe. We all want to be Happy, being a **Proton** to attract happiness (positive (+) energy) and emulate **a Being of positive (+) force** will make you happy. This positive energy will fuel and make you a stronger **Proton** and according to the **Law of Attraction** the happier you are the more happiness and positive (+) energy you will attract; because you are only focusing on being happy which will continue to manifest whether you believe it or not. But we also need to remember Jesus who showed that even with all of the power of the Universe (God) here on Earth , one can humble themselves, contain that power, and use this power to be a Strong Force of Good. We all forget that Jesus was a badass. We have this image that Jesus was only a peaceful being that had never showed anger or frustration. Well open your eyes dumb-asses. In the **New Testament** he was described as, "**Teaching with Authority**". Authority means when he was talkin' he didn't mess around. He couldn't stand all the priests and the so called "powerful" of society. How 'bout when he saw the gambling in the temple? Yea he wasn't so peaceful then was he? All's I'm trying to show is that there is so much more power in being Good (being a **Proton**) than we realize. Like Jesus, we need to humble ourselves before God. We do this by Changing our **Soul** to the **Nucleus**, being like Dad (the **Proton**) and Jesus (the

Neutron). The **Neutron** has a Neutral, dormant charge (No charge). The combination of the **Neutron** and **Proton** makes the **Nucleus**. Becoming like the **Nucleus** makes you a very **Humble, Powerful force of Energy** (what God **expects** from us). Once you become like the **Nucleus** all of the **Protons** and **Electrons** (Your **World**, Your **Atom**, Your **Garden of Eden**) will begin to be pulled in and revolve around you and your powerful "**Spiritual Gravity**". And you won't be fazed by what the doubting haters say because you won't have any time to be mad and angry when you enjoy being happy too much. Now you're asking, "how do we become like the **Nucleus**?" It's all in the **Power of Prayer, realizing we are children, and need to give in and enjoy being God's KID**. Read the chapter about effectively and appropriately using your **iGod** (**Soul**).

My name is Tyler James (T.J.), I'm 20 years old pursuing a business degree with minors in psychology and philosophy. I'd be majoring in the 2 latter but with the minimal job market for those 2 subjects I guess I have to fall in society's assembly line and take the business route. I'm not the greatest writer and I'm not aiming to be the next Emerson. I don't expect my book to be the best, most excellent writing you've ever seen, I'm just a **Child of God** with big **thoughts** that need to be shared with the World and I pray that God's true followers will hear what I have to say; what God wants me to say. It's time to bring power to the **righteous men and women** of the Universe that truly make it work (Positive(+) energy). And bring power back to God and Jesus (Positive (+) energy); transfer the power from the negative (-) energy (South Pole) of the world to the positive (+) energy (North Pole).

The Number 3: Welcome to Worldbook

The next chapter is the most important **Parallel** that God has left us to find. But, before you read about that you have to understand the importance of the number 3. This is the most important number in the Bible and too God. Obviously it's important to God because he is made up of 3 parts:

1. Father
2. Son
3. Holy Spirit

Now, here are a few examples of 3 in our world:

Once again, at the basis of science the **Atom** is made of 3 parts:

1. Proton
2. Neutron
3. Electron

There are 3 states of matter:

1. Solid
2. Liquid
3. Gas

The Earth is the 3rd planet from the sun, there are 3 primary colors, we live in a 3-Dimensional World, and "it takes 3 to tango" (just kidding). I will be talking about the most important thing in nature that is made up in 3 in a second.

My theory on why the number 3 is so important to God is based on the very definition of himself. He calls himself the Alpha and Omega, or the First and the Last. I think this name is referring to the concept of a story. Every story has a beginning, middle, and an end. God **Began** the Universe and will bring the **End** to it.

I believe that Sending Jesus to Earth would be considered the Middle, and everything between (Us) the Beginning and the End makes up the story of Earth or our existence. I think that Jesus coming to Earth is the climax of the story or lesson you could say.

Even though this lesson is for Us, Jesus showed God that there needs to be **compassion** for Mankind. He showed that even in the face of evil, one can still exemplify God (being a powerful [(**Proton** (+)] and contain that power (**neutral**) even in the time when Jesus should've been furious and used that power). He exemplified **The Nucleus** (**humble** and **powerful**) we all need to become like.

This makes sense considering in Revelations God states, "And if anyone's name was not found written in the **Book of Life**, he was thrown into the lake of fire." (Revelation 20:15). So basically, your part in the story of the world dictates whether you will be recorded in the book of life/be accepted into Heaven (be the Protagonist or the Antagonist). We all watch movies and shows and say I wish that would happen to me. Well the **Book of Life** is the largest movie script with insane amounts of characters in it. Think about it, everyone is unique, each of us with different, specific roles to play all of which must combine to contribute to God's story, whether they are aware of the part they are playing or not. And if you don't make an effort in God's eyes, you won't be a part of the story of Earth (**Book of Life**) and won't be accepted into Heaven.

So if you're asking, "how do I get my story to God?" **Then first stop and thank Jesus for creating the biggest Social Network on the planet**… **Worldbook**. Yep, **Worldbook**. You can create your profile anytime. But, the only catch is you must present all of your "pictures" and "posts" to God haha. To access your **Worldbook** account you need to discover and properly utilize your **iGod** (**Soul**). Skip ahead a few chapters to find out how to setup and start using your **iGod** and **Worldbook** today.

I believe that my part of the "**Book of Life**" (**Worldbook**) is writing this book. I've always had feelings of being different and that I **had** to do something. The more I write this book, I can literally feel weight being lifted off of me, as well as off of my Conscious/Soul. I'm not saying you have to go to the extreme like this to find/please God, but (sounds cliché) your Heart knows what God expects from you. Your part for God may be as simple as just seeking him out and trying to learn about and love him. Nothing makes God (or any parent for that matter) happier than when one of His children truly wants to seek Him (them) out and love them. But, do not just go to church regularly and expect him to be happy with that. I see the word **church** paralleled to the word **crutch**. If you only rely on church to make a relationship with God that is not at all what God wants you to do. He wants it to be a personal relationship that you, on your own, take time to seek him out. For me, I felt like God has always wanted me to do something for him and once again I feel that I am doing it. When I started writing these thoughts down, I took on the idea that literally God could talk to me/us. And after that, I started seeing signs that kept encouraging me (which also further fueled my episode) to keep going, that made me feel like I was actually doing something important. I have to refer back and thank, thank, thank Scott Mescudi (Kid Cudi) for his guidance and strength through all of this. Listen to his song "Know Why". The song is a prayer that Scott is having with God. He states:

> "I thought my mind was cappin'
> Until I open my eyes
> And see what finally happened for me
> I know you made me different for a reason God
> I think I know why (why)
> I know you put me through it for a reason God
> I think I know why (why)."

For the longest time I listened to this song and tried to find understanding of why all this shit happened to me. It finally became clear to me in November 2010 when I actually started writing this, and now…I know why. So listen to this song it might help. But, just listen to yourself and you'll "know why" God put you here. Also know that God made you and he knows what your interests are, hate to break it to you but your **worldbook** account is already set-up so you better login and make sure there's nothing on there He won't like haha. So look for God in the music you like, the sports you play, or the movies you see. If you **Truly Believe** and **Truly** want to hear from God and feel his presence, just know and **Truly Believe** that he can and is always talking to you. Start looking for Him. Don't listen to your conscious thoughts, follow your actually feelings; call it an **inner compass**. If your conscious mind is preventing you then just keep telling yourself to listen to your emotions. Make it a challenge to feel and interpret your feelings. Be patient

Getting back on track, I believe that the order the Holy Trinity is stated (Father, Son, Holy Spirit) is also in the order Beginning, Middle, and End. My thought on this is the Father comes before the Son and the

Holy Spirit (Heaven) comes after both. Just like the Bible teaches us **Old Testament** (Father), **New Testament** (Son), with the **Holy Spirit** coming next. That's where you come into play ladies.

So if the number 3 is important that means that the shape of triangles is very important. There are a few important triangles that God wants us to see. First, the Holy Trinity:

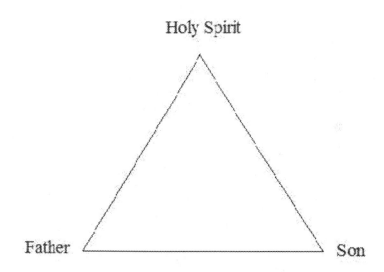

Next is the Triangle for Creation here on Earth:

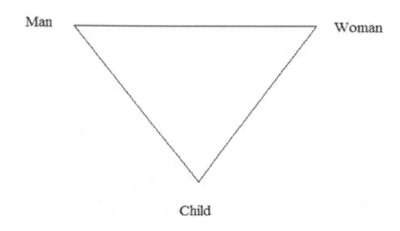

We know that God is our Creator so we can infer that the Holy Trinity Triangle (Spiritual Creation) comes first and made Mankind. And obviously we know that we are created from the Triangle of Creation on Earth (Physical). So, combine the 2 and you get the "Star of David":

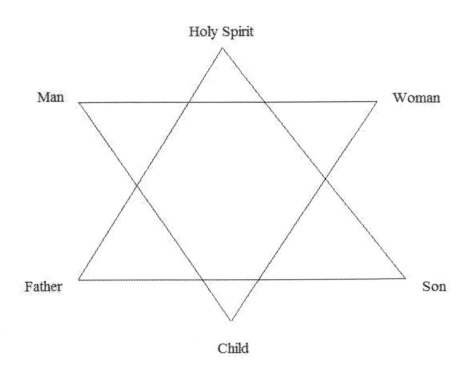

Reading about the Star of David I read something saying that the Star of David was used to signify Jewish people in both Secular (Political) and Religious ways. Once again could this be a **Parallel** for us to see? I really think it could. This shows the combination of 2 different triangles (God creating Us and Us creating Us) creating a symbol used to represent a large group of people in both "Church and State" parts of society. And by using its representation in both Church and State, God is trying to tell us that 2 views (2 different triangles) can be brought into one (Science/Religion). For example the Creation Triangle above; it combines the Spiritual (Religion) and Physical (Science) triangles of creation to form 1 symbol that can explain our creation both spiritually and physically.

Lastly the pathway to God is given to man as a Triangle:

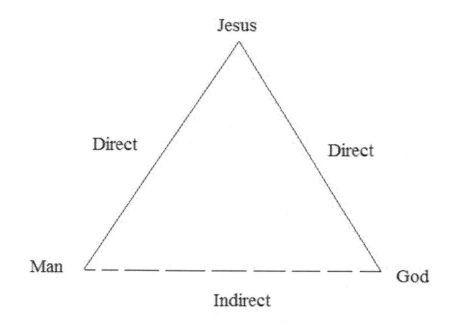

Parallel of Jesus and Water

This is my most proud theory that I figured out; because, this theory combines the two ideas of the importance of 3 from the parallels of Science and Religion. Just to recap, like I said before, Jesus taught his lessons with examples from Nature. So I thought about that for awhile and started to make some connections. If we think about Jesus and his importance to religion we can layout most of the reasons for why he is praised so highly:

1. He is needed for survival after death (Eternal life).
2. His **Ascension** and **Descending** from Heaven.
3. His cleansing of sins.

Now let's look at what makes up, and dictates Jesus.

1. He is the Holy Trinity (3 parts)
2. His **Ascension** and **Descending** is determined by God who is also the Holy Trinity (3 parts).

Next let's look at the importance of Water:

1. Needed for survival on Earth.

2. Water **Ascends** to the clouds ("Heaven") and **Descends** back to Earth.

3. Water is what we cleanse are body with when dirty. Also, we are baptized with Water to rid **Original sin**.

Now let's look at what makes up and dictates Water:

1. There are 2 Hydrogen molecules and 1 Oxygen molecule (I see the 2 Hydrogen molecules as the Father and Son, and the Oxygen molecule as the Holy Spirit); 3 parts.

2. Water's **Ascension** and **Descension** is governed by the Water Cycle: Evaporation, Condensation, and Precipitation (3 parts).

And obviously Jesus was praised for his numerous miracles performed during his time here on Earth. The only thing that you could compare this to with Water would be that Water is the main necessity that is needed to sustain the "miracle" of life. Especially considering how rare the existence of life is in the Universe, I'd consider Water a miracle worker in itself by sustaining by far the most unique part of our universe… Us.

It is almost scary to think about when you see the same characteristics between the two. So what could this mean? Does God want us to praise Jesus and Water? I think we need to take a step back and think about what God and Jesus wanted the Disciples to do after Jesus left this planet. Jesus told his Disciples that they were to spread his word around the world. Now-a -days this job is dubbed to Missionaries to travel the world and preach the word of God. But most of the places that they are preaching to and trying to convert have extremely unhealthy environments. The main thing these places lack is clean Water. According to Abraham Maslow's "Hierarchy of Needs", humans must first satisfy physiological needs before beginning to seek one's full potential/capabilities. For example, someone might want to strive to be a good athlete or an artist. But, before you can begin to strive for those things, simple necessities: food, Water, and shelter must be taken care of first (Basic needs for survival).

So, if these places that lack clean Water, with their societies and citizens only focusing on trying to survive, why would they want to hear about a story (the Bible)? It might be entertaining to them but they can't get to the top of Maslow's "Hierarchy of Needs" Pyramid and truly seek, understand, and believe in God; because, they are still at the base of the pyramid struggling to survive. So maybe God wants us to see this comparison to help them begin to **Ascend** up Maslow's pyramid.

I believe that God is trying to tell us something by this. In revelations God refers to Water as the "Water of Life", the **Key** to survival on Earth. We also know that Jesus is the **Key** for eternal life. I see this comparison of Water and Jesus as a sign from God that first the necessity of survival on Earth must be **Spread/Attained**, before the word of God and survival after death can be **Taught/Attained**. Treat Maslow's pyramid as a ladder; Physical Survival are the bottom rungs and Spiritual Maturity are the top rungs. Spreading the Bible alone to these struggling societies is like trying to reach the top rungs of the ladder without using the bottom rungs first. Maslow's Pyramid is truly **Jacob 's Ladder**.

After getting them clean Water, let them know that the blessing came from God (and maybe even show the comparison between Water and Jesus), let them decide whether they want to pursue the Christian faith and God, just like we all had the opportunity to **Decide** whether we wanted to pursue God or not. Shoving it down their throat isn't the way to do it because it is their "**Spiritual Journey**" to either seek God or not.

Going back to "Maslow's Hierarchy of Needs", you have helped satisfy a major part of their physiological needs and in turn they will be more receptive and excited to hear the messages you are trying to send; because you have helped them out more than they could ever thank you for. They will see your kindness and help as a sign of grace and will want to learn about the Being that sent you to them. This blessing that you have helped them achieve will let them begin their **Ascension** up the pyramid of the "Hierarchy of Needs" or **Jacob's Ladder**. With new found health that was impeded by lack of clean Water, they will be granted more **Time** here on Earth to seek God and Jesus if they so choose and **Learn** about the Laws of Science (Earth/Mom) that make up the Earth. So our mission for God is to grant and spread Water (the "Water of Life") to the less fortunate, **then** spread His Word (the Bible), the "Key to an Afterlife".

My church started a project called "Living Water". They use the offerings and donated money to dig wells and give these struggling societies clean Water. It is starting to catch on and other churches are joining them. They showed a video of the first village they gave Water too and I was almost brought to tears from the happiness that the people showed. They were so thankful. Kids were playing in the Water and the people viewed it as a miracle. Everyone needs to follow this example and begin to do the same thing.

Returning to the parallel of Science and Religion, couldn't we **All** agree (even atheists) that these people need to be helped maybe even saved. The giving of Water is Science's job (Mom's part) to provide physical survival to these people and the Religion side of the job (Dad's part) is to come in and teach about where the gift of grace came from. So I see this as God wanting us to combine both of these views to save them here on Earth (Science) and then save them spiritually (Religion).

There are 884 Million people (1 in 8) without sufficient clean drinking Water and 3.575 million deaths a year from unclean Water related diseases. For all you unsympathetic Science lovers (Momma's boys haha), 300 million school days on average are being missed. So, in a way Science believers really need to see this **parallel** and take into account the fact that these kids/people aren't getting the opportunity to learn about anything other than basic survival. Science, show your mercy in the fact that these kids aren't being given the same opportunity to learn the things that you love and study. Help their physical survival/needs and they will want to learn about what you have to teach them. And who knows, these undeveloped/uneducated societies might possess knowledge that we don't. They could have answers to riddles that we haven't been able to figure out yet; like cancer for example (Just a thought).

We all know that Water has very destructive capabilities and I'm assuming that you are struggling with the thought of why would He do so much harm against other countries with hurricanes and tsunamis, when they are so innocent. Honestly, I struggled with this too but then came the idea that God is pointing out on the map where we need to help. Because God wants and needs help from us just like with making the Universe, we need to learn the truth about the Holy Spirit (which is the next chapter) and help God help these people. And if you can't find any sympathy to help these people just think about this; while the only thing you are struggling to decide between is getting some water or a soda or a red bull or coffee or some alcohol or a five hour energy or some Gatorade, etc... 884 million other people across the planet are struggling to decide between drinking the shit infested Water or drinking the brownish green Water

So let's start spreadin' the Water!

Assignments:

- Start at the bottom of Maslow's Pyramid **Together** (at the "basics", Science (or survival) first).
- Branch off to teach about God/Jesus.

- Branch off to teach them the theories of Science that saved them.

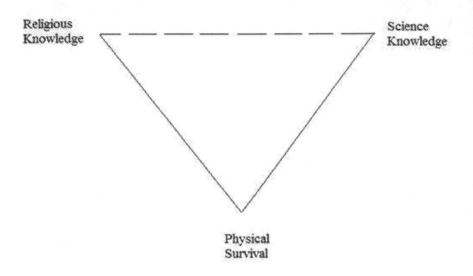

Parallel of Communion:
Discovery of our Mom

Looking further into the importance of Water, let's look at the sacrament of Communion. Communion is the eating of bread and drinking of wine in remembrance of Jesus' sacrifice for humanity. Once again I believe that this sacrament from the Last Supper goes deeper than a simple thank you to Jesus.

Obviously we can see that the wine represents the blood of Christ. We just talked about how Water is the key to survival on Earth, while appreciating and accepting the blood spilt by Jesus is the key to survival after death. This appreciation is performed by drinking the wine during communion. So in a way Jesus' blood (the wine) represents the new water for the next life. That, or water and wine are one in the same. I believe that truly Water and wine are the same in the context of Survival and God, Water being the necessity for survival here on Earth, and the appreciation of what wine represents (Jesus' sacrifice) is the key necessity for eternal life with God in Heaven.

[A little side note (Food for Thought)]:

- Jesus' first Miracle was turning Water into wine.
- Ironic that a glass of wine with a meal reduces the chance of a heart attack and stroke (Not all the time but occasionally).

For them to be one in the same means that they both would have to represent something which, would be "blood". I see wine as simply just representing the thank you part of being the "blood" of Jesus. Once again, Water is way more important in the context of Communion than we realize.

Like stated above, God refers to Water as "The Water of Life". This is obvious because without Water nothing on this planet would survive. Now to combine the Science and Religious view together again let's first look at Genesis in the Bible.

From the Garden of Eden came a river that stemmed into 4 rivers:

1. Pishon
2. Gihon
3. Tigris
4. Euphrates

Considering that these are thought to be the first rivers of the world from Eden, we can assume that they flowed to all parts of the world. And this makes sense considering that at one time all 7 continents were combined as one (Pangaea). I'm sure you can guess where I'm going with this but if not I'll further elaborate.

Now let's think about the flow of life (blood) in our body.

The Heart is composed of 4 chambers:

1. Right Atrium
2. Right Ventricle
3. Left Atrium
4. Left Ventricle

Well at least now we can see why God refers to Water as the "Water of Life", because Water is the blood of Earth. Rivers can be looked at as veins and veins looked at as rivers, it's a hard comparison to deny (Water and Blood=Parallels; Rivers and Veins=Parllalels). From this we can conclude that Water and Blood are Parallels of each other:

- Water= "Earth's blood"

Going back to the concept of Pangaea, we can look deeper into the other part of Communion, the Breaking of the Bread. This represents the splitting of bread by Jesus for us to eat so we can appreciate and except what his body had to endure for Our sake. Once again, the bread means way more than just a simple thank you to Jesus. Before Jesus breaks the bread he states, "This is my **Body** which is given up to **You**." Receiving (Eating) the bread is a sign of Appreciation for what Jesus did for us. But just like Water representing the blood of the Earth, the bread represents the **Land mass of Earth**, which at the beginning of time was combined as one (Pangaea). So if the bread represents the land, than the splitting of the bread represents the split (Continental Drift) of Pangaea into our 7 continents. Here is the Wife of God and our Mom we have all been looking for.

Earth's 7 continents are the 7 spirits of God that are seen in Revelations as the 7 lamp stands (that's just speculation).

So, with these comparisons between Communion and Earth, what could God be trying to show us by this **Parallel**? First, we already know the religious reason for Communion is to thank and exalt Jesus for his Sacrifice. But, now we have to see Earth as a living **Being** (Mom) that has been given to us (Jesus- "My body which is given up to you.") and also thank/appreciate Her (thank/appreciate Women).

But what God is angry about is the fact that we don't see Earth as our Mother anymore and have been seduced by Her, being consumed by Her pleasures (Sin). Mankind has lost sight of the fact that **EVERYTHING** comes from Our Father God. Because of this Mankind has become weak physically and weak willed. We depend on Earth for health, happiness, and guidance. We have lost respect and love for our Father the rightful deserving one of our Praise. Because, depending on and fearing the Mother is what leads to abnormalities in psychology. And depending on and fearing Mother Earth is what infuriates our Dad, God. So treat and Love the Earth like the Mom she is and don't be consumed by the temptations of Her pleasures. Yes, Our time here is meant to be fun, but first you must humble yourself before the Lord Our God and thank him and Jesus for Every single thing that makes you happy in your life; from Your House or Car to your very next breath. I can't emphasize enough and heed my Words:

EVERYTHING COMES FROM JESUS AND OUR FATHER.

Anyway to further show Earth as Our Mom, let's just look at her as a Mom. Obviously from plants and vegetation we can see that their seeds are planted into mother Earth and she gives them the necessities to grow and live. From her all plants and animals will grow. If we think about the concept of getting into Heaven; it means that technically we are still "developing" preparing for our rebirth into Heaven. This means that the Bible is meant to mold us into the Children of God we are (mold our Spirit). So, technically we are still in Our Mother's womb (Earth) still developing and trying to earn our way into Heaven.

Secondly, the Science view is that Earth is a living **Body** that was given to man. Either way, no matter what your belief about the existence of Earth is, we have to be Thankful and admit the fact that we are here and have been blessed with (given) the Miracle of Life. To sum it up I see God as the Body (Land) of Earth (Food we eat), Jesus as the Blood (Water) of Earth, and the Holy Spirit as the air we breathe (Oxygen), 3 main components of survival and Earth. I know that it sound's contradicting about the land being our Mom and God, just here me out. We have to remember a couple things. God is a single Being and **Everything** comes from him, which means Earth comes from him. Once again, Jesus stated at the last supper, "This is my body that is given up to you." God gave up his body for us to choose to exalt and thank him for it or not. And we do this first by thanking Jesus for showing us to be thankful to our Dad.

So what created Pangaea and the split? This goes back to the Fall from Eden of Adam, Eve, and Lucifer. I think that the Asteroid that hit the Earth was Adam, Eve, and Lucifer. This is the "Fall of Man". When we fell we set apart Pangaea and the Spirits of God.

Now looking at the Sacrifice Jesus had to make for Us represents something of its own. He not only had to wash away and feel the pain of our sins against God, but also (more than likely) had to wash away the future torture that would be endured by Earth (God's "Body") from then until now. I see Jesus' Sacrifice as a bigger favor than we can ever, ever, ever ("... I didn't have enough ever's memorized."- Brian Regan) thank him for what he did. And right there is where Earth our Mom also needs to thank Jesus. We talked earlier about how teachings of the Father came with the **Old Testament** followed by teachings of the Son from the **New Testament**. We know that when we pray we say Father, Son, Holy Spirit. So now we can see that we are still waiting for the "**Spirit**" to come. There are 7 spirits of God and 7 continents, both of which all used to be 1 (combine to be 1 **Spirit** again someday). So the Spirit is here on Earth and already in all of us, our **Soul** (**iGod**).

The reason that Earth should thank Jesus is Jesus showed Us and God that we have to be **compassionate**, thankful, and peaceful Beings. Just like the Love a mother shows their child, "only a mother could love that face". We (especially men) all forget that we contain a small chromosome of the other sex. "Real Men don't cry." Ok so are Men that do cry "Fake Men"? This is the lesson of the **Holy Spirit** we have all been waiting for. If the lesson would have gone **Father**, **Holy Spirit**, **Son** it would make more sense and easier to see. We talked about how God needs a Woman (Science) to create the Universe and all the species of Earth, because think about it Jesus came from God and wasn't tainted by Man's genetics, that means that Jesus came from God (Dad) and was born onto Earth (the Mother of Mankind). I believe the **Holy Spirit's** lesson is swallowing Our pride and admitting that help is needed (Men admitting women are needed also to create a child). To show this Spirit we must realize that even though we create more Men and Women here we are all created by God. We have to realize that our parents here only represent the "training wheels" for development and after that we are just Men and Women of God (**Children**).

Proper **Holy Spirit** (=) **Compassion** (feeling our emotions (+) admitting we need help creating a baby with the help of a Women, along with admitting there is an outside force that created us and the Universe).

Let's show the **Atom** of the Universe and God.

Original **Atom** (the Universe):

1. God (**Proton**)
2. Son/Earth/Mankind (the **Nucleus**)
3. Science/Mom (**Electron**)

The **Atom** of Earth itself, the Original Creation of Mom (Science) and Dad (God);

1. Sun (God)
2. Earth (Jesus)
3. Moon (Mom)

The **Atom** of Mankind:

1. North Pole (God/Heaven)
2. Mankind (**Potential, Neutral Energy**)
3. South Pole (Satan/Hell)

It's time to admit that the **Soul** and **Prayer** are real and very powerful, which up until now have been used for **Evil not Good**. So if these things are all real than we need to change our perception of Earth. Think about the **Earth as an extreme Social Network** like facebook, once again, "**Worldbook**", and we are like an **iPhone** that can connect to the network. We connect to the network (**Worldbook**) with our **Soul** (**iGod**). We talked earlier about positive (+) and negative (-) energy pulling us all between good and evil. So if we can feel the pull of good and evil between all of us, that means there is a push and pull we feel between Heaven and Hell. We also talked about the Earth being a magnet with the North and South Pole. North Pole is obviously Heaven and the South Pole is Hell. Think of these 2 as cell phone towers. You can send your prayers to either pole, and can access and attain the power of either; just a warning to all you Anti-Christ's, it is scientifically proven and tested that an affirmative thought is 10-100% more powerful than a negative (-) thought, your gunna get crushed. We access the North Pole (Heaven) by being good (a **Proton**) and sending our prayer's to God and Jesus. Once you start to feel good, according to the Law of Attraction, more good will find you; and if your goal (like mine) is to find God and Jesus to establish a **real** connection with them, they will find you, this is according to the Bible where Jesus says, "Ask and you shall receive", "Knock and I will answer", etc. Also, this is in accordance with the Law of Attraction itself which states that what you think about and feel about the most will come and find you also (Neutral task for both you and God). When you're in a good mood everything seems to be going good. That's because you are "plugged into" "**Worldbook**" and feeling good. Those "good feelings" are what is being heard by God and Jesus. So, you are inadvertently praying 24/7. This makes sense considering that God is the Omniscient, All Knowing Being he is. So you better get a better grasp and understanding the power of prayer. Same things apply the South Pole and the **Electrons**, except they will be met with misery, doubt, fear, and hate (doesn't sound to fun). You are "plugged in" to "**Worldbook**" by your **iGod**. No matter if you realize this or not you are constantly plugging and unplugging from the network ("**Worldbook**"). This is where "Good" or "Bad" days come from. I call the **Soul** the **iGod** because we have to remember that we are God's **CHILDREN** which means we must have the **Spirit of a Child** (Imagination, have fun with life!!!). And if you still are struggling with this remember that the Earth is our Mom. The North and South Pole are hear ears. Every feeling and thought is filtered through her to God. You could say that Mom reports to Dad on how we are doing. This seems like most families anyways today, the Dad's are out working only concerned with their job and providing for the family. This leaves Mom stuck dealing with the kids emotional problems and issues. Dad's are naturally distant individuals when it comes to their children anyway so it makes sense that Mother Earth has to report all of their children's bitching to the Father.

Now we can see how insanely difficult Jesus' Sacrifice was. He only Sacrificed himself so that we could all one day gain the same connection that he did with God. So Jesus is the creator of "**Worldbook**" and prayer. I compare His Sacrifice too owning a misbehaving, family dog. Let's say that the family Son (Jesus) brings home a Dog (Mankind) and the dog does nothing but terrorize and destroy his new house. Obviously, not appreciative of the shelter he is given, the Dad (God) gets pissed at the Dog and wants to kill it or get it out of the house. Even though the Dog has shown nothing to deserve the home and kindness, the Son still has hope in the Dog and doesn't want him to die or get thrown out. The Dad makes a deal with the Son that if he keeps it he would have to suffer the consequences of the Dog, or get rid of it. For some reason the Son has so much compassion for the Dog that he decides to keep it and receive the punishment that should rightfully be put on the Dog.

So yes, I believe that we are no more than Jesus' pets and he is the only reason that God hasn't put humanity through the suffering it deserves or wipe us **All** off the face of the Earth. God would destroy us but would never destroy Earth, it's his favorite and most prized creation (It's our Mom to nurse Mankind for the Second birth (Rebirth into Heaven). Earth is also Dad's (God) and Mom's (Science) First son you could say). And if you think me saying we deserve suffering is drastic, take a second and think about all the Shit that we do to each other and to this planet we've been blessed with (given). And if you wunna try and say, "I'm a good person I don't do bad". Well even if that is somehow true, suck it up, 'cause if you've ever played a sport and been on a Team you Damn well know that even if it's just one Player that messes up, the whole team pays the price. So be warned and prepare yourselves, 'cause the pain we deserve will be coming soon. And if you want to skip ahead, I have a theory that will tell you when it's coming.

Alright now calm down and let that digest a little. You don't have to agree with me, alls I'm asking is for You to just take a second and look outside. Think about the fact that you are alive and have everything here to keep you alive. So, no matter what you believe in take a second and be thankful for the Gift of Earth we have all been given. We have to except that the Earth is a living body and must show it more respect and appreciation. I know this sounds like a tree hugging plea; but if we abuse and destroy our Earth where do we expect to survive? Begin to treat the Earth like an ailing body and show it care and love and the Earth will in turn show it's appreciation to us. My Dad has always taught me since I was a kid, "Take care of your equipment and it will take care of you." So please take these **Parallels** into consideration and appreciate the gift of Earth that we have been given.

What we have learned about the **Atom** of the Holy Sacrament (=)

- The Father (**Proton**) (=) Powerful, Defensive, "Hard-Nosed".
- The Son (**Nucleus**) (=) Having the power (**Proton**) of the Father (+) Also being compassionately humble (**Neutron**) no matter how powerful you become.
- The Holy Spirit (**Electron**) (=) Being like our **Mother's**. Exemplifying a happy, loving Spirit. Being in accordance with the 10 Commandments and Jesus teaching's is all you have to worry about. It's not difficult and trust me it is fun. Jesus is the best Theopholis to ever walk this planet. That means that he is one of if not the best teacher to ever walk this planet. So if you just view it as I'm just learning how to be the best Universal person someone can be then everything becomes fun. You let

go of guilt and doubt in doing things and will just attract more happiness and positive (+) energy to you.

- Become all 3. We are all supposed to be good examples of Jesus. We are taught to be a "Christ Like figure". We are supposed to be like our Father, Brother, and Mother. A confident, powerful, humble, compassionate, loving Human Being. Amen.

Bridging the gap between Us and Us:

Like I stated at the end of the second chapter, people try to pair Religion with the wrong field of Science. Everyone wants this connection to be so complicated with someone like Albert Einstein to come in with an 8 page equation that solves it all! Why does it have to be so complicated? And if we take a step back are we expecting the right type of Science to make this long awaited connection?

I believe that trying to make the connection between Religion and Science through the fields of Mathematics and Physics will never happen or won't right now. Though they can explain the laws of Science (Mom) that God has imposed on our World, I don't believe that these are the correct concepts to apply to this dilemma. Now that we know the Earth is a living physical Being in itself (Mom), it makes more sense to try and make this connection through using Science's fields of Psychology and Neuroscience instead. Just like Religion, these fields still have much to explore. Psychology is the field of study about the systems/functioning of the brain, along with the study of the development of our physical body. Neuroscience studies the nervous system combing biology, psychology, physics, and chemistry. So if the Earth is a physical body, this means that it must also have a "brain", right? Once again I see the galaxy paralleled with the brain. If we think about the complexity of the human brain and the galaxy with all of the uncharted abilities and areas that they possess, it's easy to see these 2 are one in the same. I truly believe now that our "Milky way galaxy" is Earth's Mind. Hear me out. Like I said both the brain and the Universe have much to explore. The Earth is surrounded by protective layers, we call it the atmosphere.

It is composed of:

1. The Troposphere.
2. The Stratosphere.
3. The Mesosphere.
4. The Thermosphere.
5. And the Exosphere.

The way I see it now is that atmosphere acts as Earth's Conscious mind; earth's "protective layer" to prevent damaging effects on the Earth's physical body. This protects us from small comets, meteors, etc. This is exactly how our Conscious mind acts to protect us. It deflects the small insults or negative (-) energy we have been talking about. If we didn't have this protective barrier to block out negative (-) energy our physical bodies would deteriorate much faster than they already do; because stress is what causes sickness, physically and mentally. We need to have a strong Conscious mind just like our Mother does. The best way to strengthen this defense is by first being confident with yourself. Second, is knowing that your parents love you with all their hearts. Third, is knowing that your friends love you for who you are. And the fourth and most powerful (in my opinion) is knowing that God and Jesus love you for who you truly are. This goes back to the golf bag example we talked about in the first chapter. If you have the first and last layer of protection you will have the strongest Conscious mind or defense you could ask for. Nothing, I mean nothing will faze you and you will not fall off of the path that you and God have laid out in front of you. Jesus says in the New Testament, "Those who walk with me through life will falter, but will not fall." This is where my strength comes from. This is what you call being "Confident". Build up your confidence through finding and building up the positive (+) energy of happiness. Once you come to the realization that God and Jesus are giving you this happiness, Everything will make you happy and stronger. Just like Muse says in their song "Resistance", "Love is our Resistance." Love is our protection and will give you more "strength" and power could ever imagine.

So, in my opinion, the galaxy is literally Earth's "brain". This sounds odd but think about the power and ability that our brain contains that we have not yet discovered how to use and possess. Just like space, "the final frontier" of Science is the brain. John Horgan, a science article writer, wrote an article titled "The Brain is the Final Frontier of Science". He says that when people ask him what field of Science they should get into he suggests Neuroscience. He makes a very valid argument, "The human brain is, in a sense, the source of our most pressing social problems: war, racism, poverty, pollution and crime. According to the World Health Organization, 1.2 billion people suffer from brain disorders such as depression, schizophrenia and substance abuse. The estimated costs of these ailments to the U.S. alone exceed $400-billion, more than the costs of cancer, heart disease and AIDS combined." People don't understand how real and severe mental abnormalities are. I can attest to this because for the past 7-8 months I was thought to be Bi-Polar (which now is found to be false, Thank You God). The stigma felt by the label of an abnormality is devastating, very hindering. We have to understand these abnormalities and begin to take them serious to beat them. I believe that the key and solution to cancer and fixing all of these abnormalities is locked away in the deeper recesses of our brain that we have not yet reached; or locked away in the minds of those that have not yet been able to fully utilize them (Ailing countries with no Water).

The knowledge and abilities we haven't yet been able to reach and use in our mind is mirrored with our limited ability to see and explore the galaxy. Just like our brain, we have only "used" and discovered a small part of space (going to the moon, maybe mars too). Maybe we will discover our full capabilities when Jesus returns; but, I believe that God doesn't want us to sit and wait. God is waiting for us to access the **Full** use of our brain, which will be **paralleled** with seeing and experiencing our **Entire** galaxy and Universe. This is where "the Climb back to Eden begins. Here's an example of how powerful the human brain truly is.

In psychology we learned about people called Savants. They are autistic individuals that also have extraordinary intelligence. Merely describing their intelligence as extraordinary is the biggest understatement I've ever said in my life. They are very rare; there are only about 100 savants in the world. The reason that they are so amazing is that their entire brain devotes itself to a specific thing, with their memory having no bounds. I'm sure you all have heard of the movie "Rain Man" with Tom Cruise and Dustin Hoffman, directed by Barry Levinson. If you haven't heard of this movie this man is also referenced in "The Hangover" where Zach Galifianakis acts like Rain Man in the Casino doing the card counting at the blackjack table. The movie is based on a man named Kim Peek. At birth Kim was born mentally challenged and diagnosed as Autistic, but had extraordinary mental capabilities. He loved to be in the library and read all day. He can go through about 8 books a day if he wanted to. It takes him 8-10 seconds to flip the page in a book reading the left page with his left eye and the right page with his right eye. After reading the book he retains about 98% of the content from the book. Absolutely amazing. Research or just look on youtube for savants, the abilities of these savants have will blow you away. Another savant, Derek Paravicini, nicknamed the "Human Ipod", was diagnosed with autism at birth along with being blind. His amazing ability goes beyond being a musical genius on the piano. He only has to hear a song once (yes you heard me, once) to play it perfectly. Even if it is only hearing and playing it once the song is filed away in his memory, forever. He remembers **EVERY** single song he's heard from the piano and can play it on command at any time (I think its over 10,000 songs, no big deal haha).

Savants have fascinated me since the first time I learned about them. I thought to myself, "What if we could all use our brains to this extent?" I truly, truly believe that **we all** have the ability to be "savants", if you will. I believe this to be true just because of the fact that every person on the planet has a unique mind compared to any other. There might be some similar characteristics (interests and abilities); but, each individual has a subject or topic they can excel in more than others. For example, psychology and philosophy come to me easy and I feel like I'm pretty intelligent in each subject. Yet, when it comes to something like physics or chemistry, I would probably fail out of the class in a few weeks time (haha). My point is that I'm intelligent and talented in the areas of psychology and philosophy but not nearly as smart in other subjects. Like I said in the 2nd chapter, I'd love to pursue a career in either or both of these fields, because I **Believe** that this is what God and my mind want me to do here on Earth. Anyway, I thought about this dilemma for awhile and came to the conclusion that my mind's abilities can excel and blossom in these subjects and not others. I believe this to be accurate because:

1. I'm intrigued, interested, and enjoy these subjects.
2. I've done well in each subject.
3. I want to pursue these subjects the rest of my life.

After figuring out my own personal abilities, I came to the conclusion that every person has something their mind is wanting and waiting to start and excel in. I'm not saying limit your mind's search to mere school subject matters. The abilities your mind wants to and can excel in might have nothing to do with school. You might be skilled and love skateboarding, singing, athletics, drivin' cars, whatever you feel like you are intelligent (good) at and enjoy is what God and your mind wants you to do and accomplish, accessing and utilizing your **iGod** (**Soul**). The only thing that impedes this is **Doubt** from **Original Sin**.

If Science thinks it is so smart and that there is no God/ higher intelligent Being… How come they can't map out and replicate Free-Will? Why haven't they flown space ships to Pluto? They can point out sections of the brain where they **think** certain things take place and are happening but they can't replicate how it is being performed (Free-Will into computers).

Just like with space, they can tell you or **guesstimate** where things in the Universe are and how they work but can't replicate or get to them. We all know that there is much to be explored and discovered in Science and if you believe in God we know that we have much to learn about when it comes to His ways/intelligence. We know and can see that are technology here on Earth has pretty much reached its peak and will probably idle for awhile with little changes until a new intelligence or discovery comes along. Think back to what we talked about with technologies advancement in the 2nd and 3rd chapter. The thought of a phone, Ipod, or computer didn't appear for thousands maybe millions of years after we existed. Back then those would've been **COMPLETE IMPOSSIBILITIES**. So really, the only thing that defines what is possible or impossible is our mind. Jesus showed us that the most incomprehensible thing is possible, defying the laws of death and resurrecting on the 3rd day after being taken off of the Cross.

Since the dawn of man we have continued to prove the impossible possible. We sit and wait for someone to come and show us that something impossible can be possible. It's time we understand that the **Doubt** in our mind is the only thing separating impossibility from possibility. We define and create our own reality. It's all in our perception. Think about time. This is the biggest perception that is different between individuals. This perception is designated as either Patient or Impatient. Think about when you are having a lot of fun at a party or something. You're having such a good time you don't pay attention to the clock and 5 hours feels like 30 minutes. Paralleled with if you are going through a shitty time or sitting at work or in class, time seems to crawl by and you're stuck. It is all in how you perceive positive (+) and negative (-) energy that dictates if you will be a happy individual (**Proton**) or an unhappy individual (**Electron**). After discovering God and writing this book, I've taken this to heart and taken it very serious and have seen that truly our only hindrance that impedes us is our perception of **Doubt**.

I believe the one concept that Man wants to explain and figure out more than anything is **Time**. Everything on this planet ages and slowly deteriorates. What makes us do that? If we ate, drank, exercised, did everything to a T of how to stay healthy; eventually, we would end up dying no matter what. I believe that after the second coming of Christ the curse of Time and false perception will be lifted off of Earth. I think that God will keep his followers, party with and teach us further. I also believe that God will grant us with new knowledge and show us the far expanses of His Universe once we lose all Doubt within ourselves, between each other, and most importantly, between God.

In space we know how large it is and want to travel out and learn about it but we are contained by the impressive, but finite knowledge we currently possess. So, I look through the Psychology perspective because I then can see the Earth as God's Physical Body and the Universe as God's mind. Religion wants to understand and learn about God's knowledge which is paralleled with Science wanting to explore and learn about the galaxy and Universe. Once again the parallel of Religion and Science is seen.

Triangle of Knowledge:

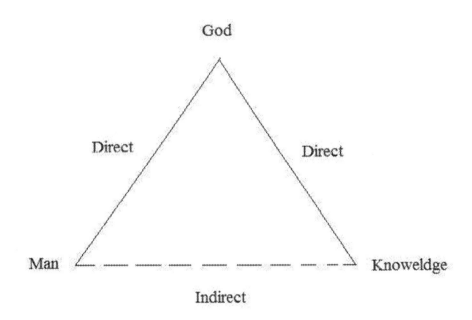

2 quick questions to those that deny God and Find comfort in Science:

- Why wouldn't you want there to be a higher, more intelligible being to Teach you more?
- And did you gain all of your knowledge by yourself without the use of a Teacher or books?

Going back to Psychology now, we can understand where and why our **Beliefs** differ. To begin, I see mankind and animals as the most complex/

efficient "machines" ever created. It's a good comparison considering we made computers in our image, only lacking free will, which makes them not as advanced as we are. While at the same time God made us in his image and we are still a step below him lacking a characteristic that he possesses, similar or paralleled to that of Free-Will. The Heart is a battery that has a limited amount of beats in its lifetime. The brain is a hard-drive that is programmed to perform many different actions, it can upload (learn) and contain (memory) new information. We need oil (Water) and fuel (Food) to keep our bodies going.

Our basic survival/bodily functions (basic instincts) are already Programmed into our Subconscious mind (hard-drive). From birth these "basic instincts" begin. For survival purposes infants have reflexes which are automatic bodily responses to a stimulus that is involuntary; that is, the person (infant in this case) has no control over this response. Here are a few examples:

1. The Rooting and Sucking Reflex- The rooting reflex causes infants to turn their head toward anything that brushes their faces. This survival reflex helps them to find food such as a nipple. When an object is near a healthy infant's lips, the infant will begin sucking immediately. This reflex also helps the child get food.

2. The Moro reflex or "Startle Response"- Occurs when a newborn is startled by a noise or sudden movement. When startled, the infant reacts by flinging the arms and legs outward and extending the head. The infant then cries loudly, drawing the arms together (Meant for times of danger).

3. The Palmar grasp reflex- When the infant's palm is touched or when a rattle or another object is placed across the palm. The infant's hands will grip tightly.

4. Swimming Reflex- An infant placed face down in a pool of water will begin to paddle and kick in a swimming motion.

So how would an infant, just born into this world with no prior knowledge, be aware to perform these reflexes if there wasn't an intellectual Being (God) to program or install these needed abilities and information?

Going back to our Conscious mind; it controls what is uploaded and contained in the Subconscious, its only job is to weigh out and make decisions (Free-Will). The Conscious mind doesn't develop for some time (Imagination Stage or our Garden of Eden), leaving us without the ability to decide what is Uploaded (no Free-Will yet). We begin with our basic instincts already Programmed in, same with animals; but unlike animals we continue our Programming stage through the first 7-10 years of life. Technically, you could call this Uploading; but, once again, considering that at such an early age the Conscious mind isn't yet developed, we don't get to decide what is being Uploaded. In turn, we are then still being Programmed. The initial Programming is done by God to form the basic instincts followed by the programming from the parents. Depending on the Child-Rearing style used by the parents, along with experienced events, molds us into the person we become (type of computer you could say). After the programming ends the Conscious mind is developed and begins to decide what is Uploaded (learned) and Contained (memory).

Whatever is learned in those years of Programming will forever be in your Subconscious. The beliefs you attain and the actions you begin to perform will stick with you your whole life. The Programming stage is where many and most "Abnormalities" stem from. Once the Conscious mind is developed it is extremely difficult to get rid of and/or attain new beliefs/actions, the Conscious Mind is your defensive shell to any unwanted energy (thoughts- negative (-), your mind deciphers what is negative (-) energy or positive (+) energy no matter what it is) from the outside world.

Just like with Religion and Science, for the kid (the **Nucleus** of the parents) to be "normal", there needs to be an equal balance between the Father [**Proton** (+)] and the Mother [**Electron** (-)]. The mother creates the Conscious mind, making them feel guilty and weary of the outside world. The Father forms the Subconscious, gives the kid a good example of the type of man to be. The Father must instill fear to get his kid's respect, but also must not forget to show compassion (the **Holy spirit**). This is the key to creating a good kid and he or she will become the **Nucleus** of the family.

The Conscious mind is where abnormalities stem from. For example, if a child is a victim of abuse, either physical, sexual, mentally or all of the above, it will take years to make even small strides in progress, let alone relieve them of the false beliefs they attained. Once the Conscious mind is developed it serves as a barrier (watchdog if you will) between the outside world and the Subconscious; deciding what gets in and what gets out. So really the absolute abnormality is the Conscious mind (Free-Will or Free-Thinking). Depending on the severity of the abnormality depends on how much or what part of the Subconscious that those false beliefs and experiences from the Conscious mind control.

Uploading (attaining/learning) **Beliefs** happens according to 2 things:

1. Conditioning (repeating) the desired ability or subject enough times to store it (file it) in the Subconscious.
2. Or the amount of people that **Believe** something to be true or correct.

In the early years, since there is no Conscious mind to think, little conditioning is needed to form **Beliefs**. In psychology this is called the "**Imagination Stage**". In this stage **Beliefs** come in and out continuously, only altering if proven not to be true. Once the Conscious mind is formed much more conditioning is needed to Upload and form **True Beliefs**; and vice versa with trying to Uninstall or Remove **Beliefs**. For example, we all go to school and learn how to do geometry. Years later even though we already went through it and can understand more difficult math, most of us would find taking a geometry test surprisingly difficult. This is because **Belief in Abilities** need constant and consistent conditioning to keep the **Belief** contained (remembered) in the Subconscious. Just like not adding fuel to a fire it will soon fizzle out. For these **Beliefs** fuel (repetition) is constantly needed. For example, N.B.A stars will shoot about 1,000 free throws a day to keep that **Ability** sharp.

I believe that there are 2 classifications of **Beliefs**. First, is the one previously stated, **Belief in Abilities**, and then there are **Beliefs in Theories**. I see **Belief in Abilities** as such things like knowledge obtained in class, being able to play the piano, any sports, etc... These types of **Beliefs** need constant conditioning in order for the skills to stay sharp and present for an extended period of time. Next, is the **Belief in Theories**, these are any **Beliefs** that are based off of opinion that can't be proven empirically. Some examples would be: God, Big Foot, Santa, U.F.Os, etc... But these beliefs are only strengthened by the number of people who think the opinion is true or not. Both of these beliefs are subject to change and questioned by a single force, **Doubt**.

Doubt stems all the way back to the **Original Sin** and reaches all the way to the unknown future, **Death**. **Death** along with the **Original Doubt in God's existence**, are the most powerful sources of **Doubt** that hinders Mankind. Sounds simplistic, but honestly **Doubt** is where failure stems from. In a literal sense, I whole heartedly believe that **Doubt** is **paralleled** with the **Devil** or satan here on Earth (**Doubt** and the **Devil** are **parallels** of each other). You can see this concept of **Doubt's** hindrance on Us in the **New Testament** from Jesus. I have 2 examples from the New Testament:

- First, when Jesus walked on Water and Peter came out to join him. Peter reached Jesus but sunk into the Water after he was scared by the unexpected gust of wind, after which Jesus said to Peter, "O you of little faith, why did you **Doubt**?" (Matt 14:22-33).
- Secondly, "Truly I say to you, if you have faith and do not **Doubt**, you will not only do what was done to the fig tree, but even if you say to this mountain, 'Be taken up and cast into the sea,' it will happen." (Matt 20:21-22).

Jesus could perform miracles because he had 0 **Doubt**. He had 0 **Doubt** in his abilities and 0 **Doubt** in God. With 0 Doubt Jesus could do whatever he wanted here on Earth. He had 0 Doubt because he didn't have any part of **Original Sin**.

I think there are 2 things that we learn about **Doubt** from the beginning of the Bible. First, the fall of Lucifer from Heaven was the introduction of the competitive spirit that all of Mankind has. Lucifer felt like he could overtake God and I believe this is why Mankind has such a competitive nature. I believe the story of Adam and Eve is the development of the **Conscious mind** and **Doubt** we see in Mankind. After they ate the apple, Adam and Eve realized that they were naked and were ashamed of it. Once we grow up, just like Adam and Eve, we **Doubted** God for leaving Us naked and **thought** (**Consciously**) we had the solution to defeat that **<u>Doubt</u>** by clothing ourselves. Aside from Earth, Mankind is God's most proud creation. I think that Lucifer realized this and saw an opportunity to get back at God. Lucifer took advantage of the opportunity and tempted Eve with the apple. Lucifer accomplished his goal and corrupted [Loaded a Virus (**<u>Original Sin</u>**)] God's proudest creation. In a way Lucifer helped God out and pointed out the flaw that mankind has, **<u>Doubt</u>**. So, God kicked us out of the Garden of Eden to see if we can defeat this curse of **<u>Doubt</u>** that we have to fight every day. And if you defeat the **<u>Doubt</u>** between you and God here on Earth, God will reward you by allowing you back in the Garden (Heaven), you might even start planting your Garden of Eden here on Earth (like me). This is where a lot of people struggle because they don't want to wait until death to make this connection. I didn't either and that's why I wrote this book. I believe that I have accessed my **<u>Soul</u>** (**<u>iGod</u>**) and have established a real connection with God and Jesus. I believe now that once we defeat the Doubt about God and Jesus we enter Purgatory.

I'm not saying that if you ever feel **<u>Doubt</u>** that you are possessed. I'm just saying that if you think about it, having **<u>Doubt</u>** in something/anything will have an effect on you and the thing you are having **<u>Doubts</u>** about. The Conscious mind is where **<u>Doubt</u>** is felt, because the Conscious mind deals with the external world, not the Subconscious. I believe that when any **<u>True Belief</u>** is subject to **<u>Doubt</u>** (if the **<u>Doubt</u>** is strong enough) the Conscious mind will pull the ability (**<u>Belief</u>**) out of the Subconscious and make it subject to examination and questioning. For example, every time Lebron James shoots a 3 in a game, he doesn't stop and think "o.k. now I put my arm up here, get my feet right here, need this much force…" no he just follows his **<u>Belief</u>** (knowledge) in that Ability from the Subconscious and shoots the ball without thought (no use of the Conscious mind). Yes, in the beginning he has to go through that checklist and condition the ability (**Belief**) into the Subconscious; but, once it is conditioned (practiced) enough the Conscious mind isn't needed anymore to perform the ability. Think of the Conscious mind as training wheels. On the other hand, if Lebron were to consistently miss rather than consistently make his shots, the Conscious mind will become unhappy with the Subconscious' performance and will pull that ability back into the Conscious mind for questioning and examination (fixing if you will). Once again for the problem to be fixed the ability will have to be repetitiously relearned (reinstalled) back into the Subconscious.

When any **Doubt** in ability comes up you can see it can lead to Stress or Depression. Because, along with the **Doubt** of the action comes the **Doubt** of the performer (you). If the problem is not fixed quickly the **Doubt** will start to reach further past just the ability and start to raise **Doubt** about yourself (being "self-conscious"). Obviously, this **Doubt** in oneself is known as Depression and needs to be subsided as soon as possible. My theory is that if **anything** is left in the Conscious mind for questioning for too long, it will lead to abnormalities. This is where we can see that repetitious conditioning (not number of believers) strengthens this type of **Belief**. Because, if you are **Doubting** that ability and everyone is telling you, you are doing fine, rarely will the performer find comfort in this. Because, the performer has an **Image** of how the action is correctly executed, making the shot for example. The only way to subside this **Doubt** is to recondition the ability back into the Subconscious A.S.A.P. The Conscious mind is the Coach of the brain; keep him happy, everything is smooth sailin', if not, better get practicing.

This is why Depression is so difficult to beat, because the **Doubts** felt are usually not empirically based and it is difficult to find a way to recondition good thoughts and self-esteem back into the Subconscious to strengthen up the Conscious defense. If you are feeling depressed and feel like you're trapped in your Conscious, I've been there, it sucks. My advice is give writing a shot. Take those thoughts and write out what your mind is trying to say. Get to the beginning source of your problems. Writing your thoughts (your feelings) out is better than talking about them; because writing them out gives you the chance to read and reflect on them. Plus, just trying to reason within yourself about the problem doesn't get the thought out of your head, only puts it on repeat, letting it circle around and around in your head, strengthening it in your Conscious to mess up your Subconscious and your **Soul** or **iGod**. If you write it out you're literally getting that thought out of your head and on paper. It might not instantly get rid of the thought but, trust me, it's better than just leaving it in your Conscious mind. Give it a try, you might feel better. Writing this book has alleviated my Conscious mind and put me at peace with myself and my life, Thank You God.

Belief inTheories:
Reverse Santa Effect

Now, **Doubt's** effects on **Belief in Theories**. These beliefs are always subject to **Doubt**, so then how can they be **True Belief**? This reason alone is why strength in numbers of the **belief** is needed rather than conditioning. With lack of empirical evidence on either side, people have to base the gravity of their opinion (or **Belief**) on the number of people who also believe in it. This goes back to Religion and Science having equal positive (+) energies from the number of people they have involved in each.

The only way that an actual **True Belief** about a theory is formed in the Subconscious is if something like a Miracle happens. If witnessed, anything that defies the Natural Law's of our World will blow right past the Conscious mind and form a Belief in the Subconscious. For example if someone were to see a U.F.O land in front of them, the Conscious mind has no time, and no grounds to make a decision on its existence or not. Now, if events like this occur, it will only be to an individual or small group of people, making the number of believers too small to convince everyone about that Theory. But, if an entire country is invaded by U.F.Os (or Hitler for example) the number of people is much greater, making the strength in that **belief** much stronger. I see the way to beat **Doubt** is to have Disciples in that Belief (Number of people). I see this to be true when looking at the word that comes at the end of a prayer, "Amen". I see Amen as standing for:

- **["A"] group of ["Men"] can do anything together"**.

Now it's time to look at the strength of Belief in Religion.

Most of us are raised on a certain Religious **Belief** system growing up. The problem I have with Religion is that with its **Beliefs** it brings so much **judgment** about other religions, people, and societies, further fueling **Original Sin**. The only reason is because of the lack of desired empirical evidence. This lack of empirical evidence creates a big insecurity making people very defensive about their **Beliefs**. This insecurity is where all of this **judgment** and **segregation** comes from. Religion today seems like it is an oxymoron, trying to promote peace and good, all the while condemning other religions for what they **believe**. Almost like a business scared to lose customers to competitors by trying to say, "O their products are shitty and don't worry, they're going out of business soon anyway". This frustrates me more than anything because going back to the concept of **Belief in Theories**, all Religions are based on **theory** and **opinion** with no empirical evidence, so why do we have to argue and condemn each other for what the other's opinion is? What are we 4 years old arguing about whose Hot-Wheels car is cooler? Grow up people. Here's how Jesus teaches about **judgment** in the New Testament:

- "Do not **judge** so that you will not be **judged**. For in the way you **judge**, you will be **judged**; and by your standard of measure, it will be measured to you. Why do you look at the speck that is in your brother's eye, but do not notice the log that is in your own eye? Or how can you say to your brother,

'Let me take the speck out of your eye,' and behold, the log is in your own eye? You **hypocrite**, first take the log out of your own eye, and then you will see clearly to take the speck out of your brother's eye." (Matt 7:1-5).

Religion is a guideline to live your life by (being a Universally "good" person, a **Proton**) and gives you something to strive for (eternal life). Either way, there's nothing anyone can do about the tension between all the World's **beliefs** so I'm just going to try and shed some light on this debate from my own perspective on these beliefs.

First, I want to look at the Christian faith which I am a part of. The Christian Religion is interesting because it promotes the **Belief** between 2 people:

- First comes- Santa Clause
- Second comes- God/Jesus

Santa is a fun concept to teach kids because it really gets them in the so called "Christmas Spirit". During the Programming stage, kids are led to **believe** that a man that lives at the "North Pole" is constantly watching them, **judging** their every move, and depending on if they are "Good" or "Bad" they will get either presents or coal. It's an effective way to get good behavior out of children. Along with teaching kids about Santa, kids are taught to **believe** that another Being exists that also watches them all the time deciding if they are "Good" or "Bad", and depending on if they are good or bad they will go to Heaven (Present) or hell (Coal). In these early years Santa Clause and God are **paralleled**. Then at about 7-10 years, around the time the Conscious mind is formed, these kids are told or find out that Santa doesn't truly exist. For most kids, this revelation shatters their whole **belief system** (I cried like a baby when I found out haha). Along with this revelation of Santa not existing comes the notion that the other **believed** Being (God) doesn't exist. This is why I believe that there is so much **diversity** in Christian based societies. I **believe** that this is where atheism stems from. Think about it, the first part of our lives we are led to believe in these 2 Beings and then suddenly find out that the fun and exciting one (easier/quicker to **Truly Believe** in) is not real. And we can't understand why others can't find faith in God?

Well its simple, this revelation is presented, most of the time, after the Conscious mind is created and both Santa and God are pushed out into the Conscious mind with the overwhelming and empirical **Doubt**. Santa is discarded, but God still lingers in the debate of our Conscious because of church, the Bible, our parents, and our Christian based society. So, God was once a **True Belief** but became subject to **Doubt** (**Extreme Original Sin** you could say) and was pushed out of the Subconscious. I **believe** that this "**Reverse Santa Effect**" is the challenge for Christians. This is where each individual's "**Spiritual Journey**" begins. They can either decide that they want to **believe** in God and try and seek him out. Or they feel so betrayed and foolish for **believing** in Santa that they just see God as a mere comforting thought and another trick.

After this, I **believe** that many things are put back into the Conscious mind for questioning. I think that this is where Homosexuality and some Abnormalities stem from. The gravity of the shattered belief system could be more profound in different individuals, leading them to question other current **beliefs** they have. This is the split in the road when it comes to Christians.

I also think that Santa is the reason that our society is so advanced and has so many luxuries. After the Santa Effect, a lot of focus is taken off of Religion, leading to more focus on let's say the field of Science [;-)]. I don't see Santa as a bad thing; it just makes regaining (Reinstalling) faith in God much, much harder.

So after seeing how Christians start off their **beliefs**, how then can we say other Religions are crazy? We teach are kids to **believe** in a man passing out presents to the whole world in one night on the day we are supposed to be praising and thanking Jesus. I saw a sticker at work that said, "Keep Christ in Christmas". I thought that summed it up perfectly. Christmas isn't even a Religious holiday anymore it's all about partyin' and shellin' out presents. So after looking at the Christian Religion and seeing how there is very little **belief** and **praise** involved in it anymore; how can we say that other Religions are crazy when they are actually acting out their **True Beliefs** they have in their Religion? And how can we condemn them for how their Religion works and society functions, when they were taught all of this in the Programming stage just like we were taught about Santa? It's just the **belief's** we attained are proven not true (Santa), bringing with it **Doubt** about God's existence, while more extreme countries are never taught about a possible falsehood in their **Belief system**.

All parts of the World look at each other in astonishment and confusion on why they do certain things. I don't think that anybody takes time to think about the fact that we **All** are brought up different, **Truly Believing in different things**.

Most other religions and societies create strict Beliefs in their childhood. Unlike Christians whose **beliefs** are shaken at an early age, other Religions are taught the ways of their faith and form very strong **True Beliefs** in the Subconscious about these guidelines. **Considering that in their society it is nearly illegal** to go against those **beliefs**, of course those Religions are going to look crazy to us (if this would happen in America they would be labeled as being Schizophrenic, bi-polar, having personality disorders, you Fucking name it. My parents tried to stop me from pursuing God because they thought I was going to go insane again…How does that make any sense if we all want our children to **believe** in God?) And coming from other countries perspectives, how crazy do you think they think we are for getting our children to **believe** in Santa and not focus at all on our Religions (Christians) actual basis, God and Jesus?

I see the problem between societies and Religions as being in the same category as Psychological Abnormalities. We try to label them as crazy, and they do the same saying we are crazy. So if everyone in the world is pointing fingers at one another thinking the other is crazy, who's the Psychiatrist deciding who's really crazy or not? It has to be God.

Going back to Revelations, It states, "And before the throne there was something like a sea of glass, like crystal." So while on his throne God has to look down through this "sea of glass" to see the whole world. We know that God is the Purest form a Being can be and we also see White Light as being Pure. Technically, God is made up of 3 Parts (the Holy Trinity) so he isn't technically "Pure". Pure White light like God isn't actually "Pure". When Pure Light is passed through a prism it is seen that it is not necessarily "Pure" but is made up of different colors:

- Red
- Orange
- Yellow
- Green
- Violet
- Blue

After seeing that Pure light is made up of different colors I see the "sea of glass" before God as the prism that He sees the world split into different "colors" (Religions, classes, races, sexes, etc…) you could say. I'm not saying that God isn't Pure; I'm just saying that God sees the world **subjectively** and not **objectively** like everyone **believes** it is (it will remain **subjective** until Jesus' return). I think this is a better way to think about God's view of the world right now. Once again, God is Purest Being you can be but is made up of 3 separate parts (Holy Trinity). I see the different Religions as the different colors that form the spectrum of God, the spectrum He sees through the "Sea of Glass". They all combine to form God but each has a **different "color"** that leads to God. **We have to remember that without the other colors, Pure light can't exist**.

For example, blue can see the Pure light. Blue also sees the other colors thinking they can see the Pure light. Blue gets mad because he **believes** that blue is the only way you can see the Pure light; while red, orange and the rest aren't looking at anything. Not realizing they are all looking at the same Pure light, they remain segregated thinking their color is the only way to get to the Pure light. The colors also don't realize that **they all** combine to make the Pure light. I think this is exactly the same thing that is wrong with opposing Religions. Each Religion thinks that their way of seeing God is right and all others are wrong, all the while they are all looking at the same God just from a different perspective (color). This also makes sense considering that we are **All** God's children that "make up" his family. The only wrinkle in this is Jesus being the doorway to Heaven. Once again we all need to understand that being raised not believing in Jesus makes it difficult to get people to agree to that. So we need to understand that we are all praising the same God and regardless of if others want to praise Jesus or not, that is up for God to **judge** them on whether they get into Heaven or not, not you.

We are all God's kids, he's our Dad. No Dad likes to see his kid's fight over stupid shit like opinion. The world is a big house and we are a big family. Some of the kids think soccer is the way to go and others think football is the way to go. It is a matter of opinion on which is better, just like which Religion is best to live your life by. We all strive to be better people through it, in every Religion. So just like combining the 2 views of Science and Religion, why is it so crazy to combine the Religions, learn about them all and take the benefits of them and live our life by that? I can't wait to read the Qur'an, learn how to meditate, and learn about other Religions. Because I believe that everything: all Religions, Religion and Science, all add up to = God. To try and fix things we might have to do something that's going to be a little uncomfortable for everyone, **change**. Everyone wants the change to be the way that they see it and don't understand that maybe their way isn't the way to do it. Why does everything have to be just 1 way? Like I stated earlier a man and a woman are needed to make a child. Shouldn't this be a good enough example to show us that at least 2 different things can work together to form something magnificent? Do you live life with only 1 eye open? If you do you're missing out on the other half of life. So, let's open both eyes up and see the World through more than just a single, constraining perspective.

A better example would be all the different types of government we have. Each government has good and bad things about it. Aside from a Dictatorship each government can lead an orderly productive society. So with each having its own pro's and con's, there is no Universally perfect government. For instance, in America there is a big segregation between Republicans and Democrats. Each side has valid, good ideas, so why not just do the sensible thing and combine the benefits of both, it's that simple. If these economic times are so bad, why not just change what needs to be changed for the betterment of the people and the country? Isn't that your job? And 14 trillion dollars in debt? When did we switch to monopoly money? And if we're that far in debt how come the countries we owe haven't come beat our ass for it? Just curious. And if you think that "combining" the good ideas and benefits from both the Republican party and Democrat party will lead to a Dictatorship. Well we already have checks and balances between 3 branches of government to prevent that. When did America switch to the United States of Democrats or Republicans? Last time I checked we are all **Americans**. Obama's on the right track right now **trying to work together** with the Republicans. At least we know that God is pleased with the Republicans since they all act like children, not even giving Obama an ear to listen to what he has to say; all because there is a Democrat in the White House? Grow up guys this isn't a beauty contest, you are trying to fix a broken country and World right now. But I guess you should wait until you guys win again so that you can come in and "Save" the country. Well obviously, Republicans and Democrats trying to work separate is not going to get us very far. We need to Unite as a country to fix our problems so we can then be a further example to the world of how to be a sufficient country. Because I guarantee you North Korea or Iran or some country is waiting for us to slip up so they can get their shot at Us. Meet in the middle as Americans; combine our positive (+) forces coming to Neutral agreements. Make America once again the powerful **Nucleus** of the World we once were. It's time for the **Original Sin** of **Judgment** and **Segregation** to be washed away from America and then the World. Obama, If you need some help with education reform let me know, you could use some youth in the image **to help**. Let's all get involved.

So, if we want Our world to run sufficiently and productively; and if we to discover **Our** God **we all** have to come together and combine just like all the colors of light have to come together and combine to make Pure light.

And does **<u>condemning</u>** and **<u>judging</u>** others make you a good person? No, so in a way, Religion counteracts itself further fueling the **<u>Original Sin</u>** that put us here in the first place. It's time to grow up and join together.

Welcome to Worldbook:
The Start to my Revelation, my iGod

One of my friends recently showed me a video on youtube about the band 30 Seconds to Mars. The video is about one of their songs called "Closer to the Edge". The video is a mini documentary from their tours and concerts around the world. The video interviews some of their fans. One of the girls they interviewed stated, "Some people believe in God, I believe in music, some people pray I turn up the radio." I think a lot of the time this is how we all feel. Everyone has an emotional connection to the music they listen too. I know when I'm upset music is really the only thing that helps me clear my mind.

There is one genre however that most people don't turn to for consoling when feeling down or emotional; that genre is rap. Rappers want to come across as "raw", "gangsta", being a "thug", basically trying to get the message across that they have no such thing as emotion. Because of those reasons I was never a big fan of rap. There seemed to be no **passion** or **thought** going into the music just rambling on about how badass they are. Scotte Mescudi is bringing about the **Second coming of Romanticism in music** (necessity to access your **iGod**).

As soon as I heard Scott Mescudi (Kid Cudi) for the first time I knew that rap/hip-hop (maybe all music) was about to be heading in a new direction. "The Romantic artist exalted instinctive feelings- not those of the masses, but individual, personal ones." (Wright, 230). This quote describes Kid Cudi to a T. Most people don't like Kid Cudi because they expect him to be a hard-core rapper, basically expecting him to give into peer pressure and become the stereotype. But, I don't think people really take time to understand what he is trying to accomplish and don't take the time to listen to what he is trying to say. He knows that he is trying to change the rap game.

What people have to understand is that Kid Cudi is not just a rapper; the man is the definition of an artist. Clive Bell (artist/philosopher) states, "The starting point for all systems of aesthetics must be the personal experience of a peculiar emotion. The objects that provoke this emotion we call works of art." (Bell, 402). The emotion he's talking about, he calls the "Aesthetic Emotion". He believes that for something to be a piece of art, this emotion needs to be swayed somehow. This goes back to the thought of the Law of Attraction. Aesthetic is paralleled with Static. That Static "Emotion" is the frequency you are sending to God. That is exactly what Kid Cudi's music is about and does to the listener. So, Scott Mescudi I must thank you for leading me to God; your music man got me through the 2 hardest years of my life, and inspired me to write this book.

Everything about Cudi's music is different. From the sound of the music in the background to the mix of him rapping, singing, humming (only way I know how to describe it), even to the words and messages of his songs; everything about him and his music is different. After hearing some of his songs you would have a very difficult time trying to pair him with a specific genre. You can't put him in rap because his songs are not all solely based on rapping alone. And you can't put him in R&B because he raps in his songs and doesn't sing about how he loves a girl in a high pitched voice for 3 minutes. I believe that he is creating his own genre of music. I coined it the name "**Hip-Notic**". I think it's kind of catchy and describes his music perfectly. I'd consider B.O.B to be in this category too. Both have discovered and are effectively using there **iGod's** (**Soul's**) to empower their music, which now is going to empower a nation, the world, and most of all Jesus and God. And they aren't Jesus freaks by any means; they each went through rough times, weren't deterred and are exalting the Lord by the strength in their music.

When you listen to one of Cudi's songs, the listener is taken into his world and almost put into a trans-like state. Here's what Cudi's goal is with his music, in an interview Cudi talks about his albums, "All of these albums will be **dream sequences**... From the beginning track **you will feel like you are in a dream**." Here's what my "Enjoyment of Music" textbook had to say about the Romantic Artist, "The Romantic era was a period in which artists aspired to go beyond the mundane, to the world of **imagination** and of **dreams**." (Wright, 229). He is right, his music is something that has never been heard before. Never before has a "rapper" used Word Painting, trying to take their listeners to places of imagination (his dreams, his mind, basically his life). He mentions his albums are about his dreams. Even the structure of his albums have never been seen before, accept back in the Baroque and Classical era's in the concept of an opera. Each album is split up into 5 Acts. Each song could be looked at as separate Movements. He describes his albums as **telling a story** about himself. So really, his albums are set-up like an opera, only lacking the visual dancers on stage. So along with a totally new sound, new structure, and purpose in his albums/music, we can see that he is separating himself from everyone else and is creating a new genre, "**Hip-Notic**".

Why do I think he went left when everyone else goes right? I think that he sees how shallow rap and hip-hop are and realized that there needs to be more to music than just telling people how much fun they are having and should go beyond trying to project yourself as a badass. In his song "The Prayer" one of his verses says:

- "Sometimes I'm thinking God made me special here on purpose So all the while 'til I'm gone make my words important so If I slip away, if I die today the last thing you remember won't Be about some apple bottom jeans with the boots with the fur Baby how I dream of being free since my birth Cursed but the demons I confronted would disperse Have you ever heard of some shit so real Beyond from the heart, from the soul you can feel."

Well I've heard you and the Lord loud and clear and I'm here to help spread the message.

In an interview about his first album, Cudi says he is trying to break down the segregation between genres of music (you could say my goal with this book is to rid all of the segregation in the world). In this very song "The Prayer" Cudi begins to break down these walls between genres. The background music is from an unknown (very good band by the way) group called "Band of Horses" from their song "The Funeral". So just like Cudi is trying to bring the power of music together for the betterment of music itself; we need to follow suit and break down the walls of segregation between God and Science, for the betterment of Humanity.

Anyway these lyrics alone show how he thinks that all hip-hop is lacking any passion or feeling behind it. "No longer seen merely as entertainment, music now could point the way to previously unexplored realms of the **Spirit**." (Wright, 229). Cudi's music did just that, he awakened my **Soul** (**iGod**). So really his music along with B.O.B (along with others; they are just my 2 favorite artists) are beginning to wake up the Holy Spirit in all of us. With most music now a days, it is merely entertainment. Unless you're getting drunk and partying, there's really no other time you can actually enjoy and listen to today's music.

Lastly, "But the Romantic vision also had its dark side, and these same artists expressed a fascination with the occult, the supernatural, and the macabre." Cudi's music also goes in this direction too. In a lot of his songs he will sing about break ups and heart break (the above song "The Prayer" has a line about Heart-break). His second album is about the dark side that comes along with becoming famous and partying. So it is clear to see that Cudi is bringing Romanticism into Hip-Hop. Here's how Scott Mescudi led me to the discovery of my **<u>Soul</u>** (**<u>iGod</u>**).

Do It Alone: The Original Song ("Turned on") on my iGod

When I figured out the deeper meaning behind this song; it was the first time God spoke to me. So really, God came and found me through this song.

This is one of, if not, the first song (s) he made. It was on his demo track that Kanye West heard that got Cudi noticed. I believe that this song is his masterpiece and after understanding that it is one of his first songs, you can see from the beginning of his career he knew he was heading in a new direction (doing something for God, or **Mother Moon (Earth)** in this case). The song is about taking his music to the mainstream level, but the song goes much deeper than just that. To fully appreciate the song you need to listen to it first and see if you can find the hidden meaning in it, but either way you can still appreciate it from me just explaining it. The song starts off with sounds that sound like they are from outer space. This is a good place to take the listener because he calls himself "Moon Man" also his albums are called, "Man on the Moon". His voice the whole song keeps calm and doesn't waver or vary much at all if any.

After listening to the song for the first time I was blown away and instantly fell in love with the song. A few weeks, or a couple months, after listening to it, I remember I really started to pay attention to the words.

And that's when it hit me. Somehow I made the connection in the song. I believe the song to be a **parallel** between Kid Cudi and Jesus. Sounds crazy, and I don't want you to think that I'm saying he is the Second coming of Christ, he is just the Second coming of Romantic (emotional), actual real music. I'm not saying that at all. I believe that the song is a **parallel** of Kid Cudi and music and Jesus and Religion. While being about Scott himself I believe it also exalts Jesus. If we could've heard Jesus talk to God before he was gettin' ready to save humanity, this is how I believe the conversation would've gone.

Enjoy the discovery of my **iGod** (my **Soul**).

First Verse

He starts the song off with:

- "**These Voices** they tell me go. Why should I ever go? Man I'm so comfortable **here**. Why should I head to a place where people **live in Fear**?"

The voice's he hears is a reference to God who is believed to be the Holy Trinity, that explains the plural use of voices. Next he says, "Man I'm so comfortable here." This is referring to Heaven, but for him, **here**, means just making music for fun, not going mainstream, he is reluctant to leave home base (the Moon). The place where people live in Fear is referring to Earth. For him, Earth means the rap game. The fear he is talking about is **fear of change**, he knows his music is different and knows that people will have a hard time accepting it and won't like it; **fearing the change** that it could start, will start.

Next:

- "But see I'll never get why the **Earth is a puzzle** that I'll never fit, I'm not of their **world**."

Once again the puzzle of Earth is referring to the rap game. Just like Jesus didn't fit into the Religious puzzle of his time, neither does Cudi fit the rap game puzzle. Obviously, "I'm not of their world" clearly shows Jesus because he wasn't of our world. But, for Cudi "their world" once again means the rap game, saying he's not a stereotype rapper.

Next:

- "So why should I leave my **sanctuary**?"

Sanctuary is once again referring to Heaven or Cudi's comfort zone (the Moon). When he is asking these questions I see them as prayers to God for guidance and help. Obviously, he is scared and nervous to go so he is looking for encouragement and help.

Next:

- "How do I know that their kind will **truly hear me out**?"

"Their kind" is referring to people, such as rappers and music listeners. He wonders if his message and music will truly be heard or if he will just be subject to ridicule and be an outcast of the music world/rap game. It's obvious to see the parallel hear because I'm sure Jesus sometimes wondered the same thing, if people were actually going to listen to what he had to say.

Next:

- "Will they understand I'm **flyin' from a different route**?"

We just talked about how he is starting his own genre (**Hip-Notic**) and understandably wonders if people will accept and understand that he is different and not just a conventional rapper. Once again Jesus came in preaching and teaching in different ways than any Religion at the time and began a revolution.

Next:

- "**Pose as a Human Being**."

Pretty obvious comparison here, Jesus was God posed as a human being. But what I think Cudi is saying here is that he **poses** (seems to be) a human-being (a rapper). He poses as a rapper but is much more than that. Like I said earlier he is much more than a rapper, he is a true artist. He is an instrument of God just like we all are, excuse me, could be instruments of God (Cam Newton after he won the National Championship said, "I'm just an instrument of God and I thank him every day for my blessings." Amen brother). Anyway, Cudi's **Soul/Spirit** (**iGod**) is using his "human form" to do the job that God sent him here to do.

Next:

- "**Mother Moon** tells me that **People need my Help**."

Going back to the questions he posed to God, we can see that he takes his guidance from the Mother Moon/Earth. This is where we know that this song is about him not Jesus. Jesus listens to his Father (God) and Cudi (Mankind) listens to his Mom (Mother Moon/Earth), God and Mother Moon are paralleled in this song. "People need my help" is a reference to Jesus because he was our "savior" or saved us from sin. In this context the people described is referring to the rap game and hip-hop. He sees rap and hip-hop going in the wrong direction and needing help to get back on the right path or head in a new direction. He definitely helped me and lit the lamp in my **Soul** (**iGod**) that led me to Jesus/God that led to me writing this book.

Chorus

The chorus starts with:

- "She said I gotta Do it Alone."

These are the instructions from Mother Moon. She tells him that he will have to make this change and "help" these people (rap and hip-hop) alone. I think that God is calling all of us to do something through our Mom (Earth). The Secret to life here is conquering every **Doubt**, everything about this Earth (Mom) to seek out and find our Father. Everything here is meant to be fun, but if you get stuck in enjoying the things (**Sins**) of Earth (the Mom) and don't seek out the Father/Son to thank him for everything he has done and given to you. Then you and your **Soul (iGod)** will be scrapped. Disconnect from the Reality of this world to see and hear from God. I'm not saying, up and quit your job just learn how to pray, learn how to see, and learn how to hear from God (Literally) here on Earth, while we are still stuck in the womb of our Mother Moon/Earth.

Also in the chorus:

• ""Do it Alone…"

This is the main part of the chorus and repeats a few times over. This part of the chorus is Mother Moon singing or talking to Cudi telling him he's got to take this journey alone. After looking at the song as him as Jesus, the title of the song makes sense because Jesus had to save (help) us alone. And this voice from Mother Earth telling us we have to "Do it Alone" is a quiet voice we all ignore, a silenced whisper that sits on the particles of Oxygen we breathe in with every breath. This whisper is our Mom nudging Us out of the nest saying, "your time with me is done. It is time you seek out and be examples of your Father (God) and your brother (Jesus)." I heard this whisper and with a little reluctance of fear feeling nervous I responded to Mom saying, "Yes Mam, thank you for raising me and allowing me to have fun. Now I must become a Man; A Man of God; nothing but one of his Children. A **Spirit** (**Soul**) that shows the strength and power of the Father knowing that I am subservient to Him and his will, while having the compassionate humble nature our Brother (Jesus) exemplified for Us. This, my brothers and sisters is the true **Holy Spirit**.

<u>Second Verse</u>

The second verse of the song is where you can really see the comparison of him and Jesus, and really get the message he is trying to send.

First:

- "She said to pack my bags dawg, and never look back."

Jesus knew when he started his journey there was no going back. Cudi knows that once he takes his career mainstream there is no going back to making music the way he used to, no going back to his sanctuary and Mother Moon.

Next:

- "This is something I have to do, a hero to **<u>save the World</u>**."

Jesus had to come here to save us. Even though he is scared and nervous about starting his career in the mainstream light, he feels that this is his purpose in life and has to do this. "To save the world" means to save music and take it in the direction it needs to be going in.

Next:

- "A Hero with no girl or no family, just **<u>Sacrifice as a Friend</u>**."

Jesus obviously, didn't have a girl and not a whole lot is mentioned about his family in the Bible and his sacrifice was as a friend, almost like saying, "I'll take the bullet for you guys, just thank me later." (Thank you, thank you, thank you). Cudi's "sacrifice" as I see it is him sacrificing himself and his music to the ridicule of the music world (presenting it to God). Knowing he's different keeps him aware that **<u>with change comes fear</u>**, and **<u>with fear comes ridicule and denial of the change</u>**. Cudi is sacrificing his own image for the betterment of music.

Next:

- "And struggle is the enemy.| But **<u>weed is the remedy</u>**."

- **<u>"And if you get Lonely, Boy you can just roll up a Dutch and</u>**..."

These two lines are indicators that he is talking about himself again and not Jesus, because obviously Jesus wasn't a stoner. But, I think that he views weed as his way of finding strength again, almost like coming back to Mother Moon for reassurance. Just like how Jesus would pray to God when he would feel lonely or discouraged. I see **<u>weed</u>** as the way to first connect with our Mother to get to the Father, that's just opinion though.

Next:

- "Keep your **<u>head high</u>**."

It seems like this line should be with the last two, but I think he is meaning keep your chin up and don't get discouraged.

Next:

- "Wunna see **<u>Home look at the Sky</u>**."

"Home in the sky" is referring to Heaven in the sky. For him it means don't forget where you came from and had to go through to get here (don't forget about Mother Moon).

Lastly:

- "Remember you're **<u>not strange</u>**, but you are **<u>not the same</u>** Mane."

What he means by this is that he has to remember that he blends in well as a rapper (not strange) but he's more than that and not the same. After the last line in the verse the song goes back into the chorus.

Going back to what I was saying before about him starting his own genre, it makes sense to **<u>parallel</u>** him and Jesus. Jesus started a new Religion and Kid Cudi is starting a new genre of music. So whether you like his music or not, you have to respect what he is trying to do by bringing real emotion and passion back into music. I'm kind of biased but I believe that his music will begin a new era of music and he will be looked at as the beginning of it.

The reason I included this in the book is because I wanted to show how deep and moving music can actually be. I know I sound like an obsessed creepy fan, but his music has really guided me along and helped me through a lot of shit in my life and I have to give a thanks to him. I'm just trying to show the power that music has and how it can sway people. Your **iPod** or **iPhone** is the key to your **iGod** and **Soul**. Let the music you feel passionate about be your prayers to God and Jesus. This is the exact reason that this song was/is so important to me. When I was struggling down at Arkansas I knew I was going to have to pull myself out of this shit hole I dug myself in. I knew I was going to have to "**Do it Alone**."

Jesus taught/showed Us and God that we need to become like the Mother and be **compassionate, Love** each other like we are truly family, this is the **Holy Spirit**. I think God has seen this connection and power that comes along with music. And like I said earlier, I kept my eyes and ears open for God all around me, and music was the place I always felt like God was there with me talking to me, comforting me. I never realized it but when I was down and listening to my music, I was just letting the song pray to God for me. Once I realized that, every emotion I felt went to God right away.

When we are feeling down we all turn to music, just like the girl at the beginning of the chapter. God knows where we all turn and has connected with **Us All**, we just don't even realize it. For me I made that connection through Kid Cudi, B.O.B, My Chemical Romance, Linkin Park, Daniel Tosh, Brian Regan, basically my whole iPod. For others it might be Taylor Swift, Slipknot, or Justin Timberlake. Whoever you listen to (unless it's some satanic band) try and find God and listen for him talking to you through the song, listen to your music and open up your mind to God and let the song be the prayer he hears.

To support this connection with us established by God, He is the Creator of our Universe, and I know that when I think about the incomprehensible expanse and complexity of the Universe I'm just blown away and just in awe. Referring back to Clive Bell's "Aesthetic Emotion", my Aesthetic Emotion's are moved by the site and thought of God's knowledge and Creations. You could say that seeing God's creations moves my "Aesthetic Emotion". So if Bell has an accurate description of what **true art** is, **then God is truly an artist**. So of course it makes sense that God would try and connect with us through music and art. Maybe the "Aesthetic Emotion" we feel when listening to or looking at a piece of art is really the feeling of God's embrace. So if the "Aesthetic Emotion" is really swayed that means, then God is really an Artist as well as a Creator at the same time; combining the view of an artist painting/creating visual spectacles (God's images) and a an engineer/"scientist". I just don't understand why people never realize that God had to actually do something to Create the Universe and had to use some type of tool (s) set or machine (s) (Help). Why is it so bad to combine the 2? It's just frustrating. Anyway, when I think of God as an artist, I think God paints every day (except on cloudy days). The sky is his canvas and every time I look at the sky on a sunny day and see the beauty in it, I feel that "Aesthetic Emotion" inside of me putting me in a "State" of joy and awe. I just say to Him, "Wow thank you for the Beauty you have given this World."

So of course it makes sense that God would try and connect with us through music and art. So remember the "Aesthetic Emotion" (Static Emotion) we feel when listening to or looking at a piece of art is really the feeling of God's embrace.

Using your iGod (Soul)

This whole book I have talked a lot about the **Law of Attraction** and using your **Soul** to effectively pray. I apologize for it being somewhat sporadic and randomly sprinkled around the book. This chapter I will tie it all together and make it a little easier to understand.

My best advice is to try and get your hands on the documentary film called, "**The Secret**". I actually saw it mid-way through writing this book. The whole chapter and theory of us being magnets and making up **Atoms** came after seeing that movie. All of the theories in this book were all talking about the **Law of Attraction** I just never realized it until I saw that movie. So thank you to all of the brilliant people in that movie; changed my life.

Anyway, back to the **Law of Attraction** or as I like to call it the **Law of Prayer**. You have to come to the realization that your **Soul** (**iGod**) is a literal magnet. Your **thoughts**, **feelings**, **emotions** are the magnetic pull that you are putting out. Just like a magnet there are 2 types of pulls:
1. Positive (+) [=] Happiness and confidence
2. Negative (-) [=] Sadness, depression, anger, lonely

Next we have to go back to the definition of the **Law of Attraction** to get a better understanding of how prayer and our **iGod** works. The **Law of Attraction** is all about the power of thought and emotion. It states that whatever you think about and feel about most will manifest to that what you are thinking and feeling about. It's really not so much what you are "thinking about" it's in the emotions you are feeling about that thought. Even if you don't realize it or intend it those feelings are being recorded and sent straight to the Big Man upstairs (God). Along with going to God, those feelings are being sent out to everyone around you.

The way I think about the **iGod** is that it acts like a 2-way radio (phone if you want). It sends out messages and receives messages. It reads and sends out emotions from/to the people around you. Communication is not based solely on speaking like we think it is. **Only 7% of communication is done verbally. The other 93% is through body language**. This is absolutely amazing but makes so much sense. Within your group of friends you can tell if one of them is in a real good mood or is feeling down about something. Depending on someone's appearance (facially, clothing, walking speed/form, age, race, sex, etc..) your mind instantly registers either cool or not cool, I can see myself talking to this person or I would never talk to that person!

We see in high school kid's segregate the whole school into different classifications: jocks, emo's/gothics, nerds, thesbians, teacher or student, cool or un-cool, popular or not popular, etc… The list goes on. I believe the worst place of segregation is the Greek life system in colleges. Don't worry I'm not a hypocrite I'm rushing right now and really enjoy it. I don't however agree with their notion of "building men out of boys". So how do they build these men? Hazing, telling them no guys allowed in only girls, you have no life outside of the fraternity, and worst of all, basically being required to switch clothing to polo and Sperry's (all applies to sororities too). The reason I say "worst of all" is because this was a big reason why I left the South. I also rushed a fraternity while I was there. Being from St. Louis I was used to just loungin' around in sweats and t-shirts. I'm not saying that I don't dress up, I'm just saying that at 7 in the mornin' I'm not going to go all out to dress up for finite math, I apologize. But, what I didn't realize was how serious people in the South take being a "Southern Gentlemen" or "Southern Belle". Me and one of my pledge brothers got into a discussion about the cultural difference between St. Louis and the South. I am not joking when I tell you that my very own "pledge brother" told me that "he used to dress like me in middle school but then grew up."

I just laughed it off at the time but then I came to the realization that Fraternities and Sororities promote the segregation between High Class and Middle Class. Yes, between High Class and Middle Class (I doubt that Greek life members are even aware there is a poor class of people haha) this is where these "boys" are taught that they are above everyone on campus, we are better than the G.D.Is (basically the equivalent to the N word to a college students), we have pledge's to clean all are shit and the house so we can trash it. Along with all of this they spark up a rivalry between other fraternities for **<u>ABSOLUTELY NO REASON</u>**. Think about it, you had to go through rush to pick out fraternities that you like. If they like you then you'll get a bid between those that like you. Then you pick the one you like. After that you become a-part of the fraternity; then instantly hate every other fraternity, including the ones that you nearly just picked???? So if you didn't get the fraternity you're now in and would've picked one of the others, you would hate that one then?

Fraternities and Sororities instill this false sense of importance when in reality you are nothing but a fucking kid getting shit faced and stoned, throwing sexual morals to the wind, trashing a house that you have been given, treating your pledges like slaves (who you are in reality supposed to be setting an example for); doesn't sound very "gentlemanly" or "lady like" to me. See how well all of these "man-molding" intangibles pan out for you in the real world. You're not going to see a grown man hit a bong or do a keg stand in front of his family. You're also not going to see a grown man trash his house and expect his children (pledges) to clean it up. A real man isn't going to bring home 2 or 3 other girls home in front of his wife or when she's not there. No, **real men** understand that responsibility is on them and they have to look over themselves, their family, and the house. Real men can't skip work to get shit faced or "accidently sleep in", if they miss work they are done and the family has no support. I don't want you all to think that I view myself as some angel, I smoke weed and drink but I do it appropriately when it is o.k. and I'm not going to be missing my other obligations and responsibilities.

Right there we can see that our very school systems promote segregation. We thought that we solved the problem of segregation when we ended slavery but we've just seen that there's even segregation within each race, segregation but classes of people. Going back to Daniel Tosh and his stand up "Completely Serious", his performance was in Orange County. He said to jokes about segregation that were hilarious but were very real.

1. "So much diversity in Orange County, I mean between Upper Middle and Upper."
3. I couldn't find the actual quote, but he was talking about people saying they live in a good or safe neighborhood or town. Daniel says, "what they are really trying to say is that where I live is really segregated."

It was a funny joke but he is so right. Most white people live out in counties while most Black and Arab people live in the city. There aren't laws that say "don't come to the county" we just all naturally segregate each other. That's just looking at the segregation in America, in 1 country. Then when you widen the picture we see that there is segregation all over the fucking world. Sunni or Shiite, Jew or Arab, Christian or you name it haha, Tutsi or hutu, the list goes on but **NO ONE CARES**. People might say they care but do nothing to change it.

Recently after I started writing this book and had my revelation I have really began to change my life and who I am. The only reason I say that is because it is needed for this story. Not too long ago a friend and I went down to a huka bar. It is a place close to the city and we walked past 4 homeless people. I gave money to the first 3 and only had a 10 when we past the last person, made me feel like shit not to give him anything. Anyway, my friend was shocked and actually furious at me that I would give them money. I asked him why and he said, "they had their chance to go to school and don't deserve it." He also said that he would probably go buy drugs or alcohol. I agree with that but he also may go buy a water bottle or granola bar. I didn't agree with his statement of "having a chance". Even if they went to school the academy there probably wasn't very good and I doubt that that school could've given them the same opportunity to go to college like we have. I was just shocked that my friend was **literally angry at me** because I was just trying to be a good person and help someone out. Seems like an oxymoron.

The reason I tell this story isn't to make you think you have to give to the homeless or for you to think I'm a good person. I just thought this was funny because the very next night I was watching the movie, "Liar Liar" with Jim Carrey. There's a scene where he walks past a homeless guy who asks for money and Jim Carrey makes up an excuse for why he didn't have any money. I guarantee that everyone that watches that scene thinks the same thing, "Wow what an Ass-Hole, I wouldn't of done that, I would've been nice and given him money." That's the point of the scene, to provoke that thought. I just started laughing when I saw that and realized that that is the way most people react to a homeless person yet they sit there hypocritically telling themselves that they wouldn't do that to them.

We just never open are eyes to see that everyone, every group, every country, every continent acts as a magnet either attracting or repelling the other. This all supports the **Law of Attraction** and the thought that we are all nothing but magnets. It's that simple.

Getting back on track with our **iGod** we have to understand that our **iGod's** push or pull has a certain strength, this strength is dictated by the Confidence you exude. We all see the popular guy and think all that separates us is that they have it all with the looks, the smarts, etc; while we don't have any of those things and we can't do that. Based on the **Law of Attraction** and our discussion of **Doubt** of course you can't do it because all of your focus, thought, and emotion is on that guy and his attributes while your feelings and emotions are saying to God, yourself, and everyone around you, "I'm useless, I'm ugly, I'm not that cool, etc." So based on **Law of Attraction** those are the things that you are going to keep seeing. You are attracting all of that negative (-) energy that you are trying to prevent.

So based on God's Law of Attraction through prayer, and based on the fact that 93% of your communication is sent through body language and the emotional signals you are sending off to everyone around you; you are actually, literally telling Yourself, God, and Everyone around you, "I'm not a happy/fun person, I don't want them to come talk to me, don't come talk to me, I want to be miserable, depressed, and lonely." This was my problem. So because the Law of Attraction says Like attracts Like and what you think and feel about will manifest you are following in accordance with this Law and are, I hate to say it, asking, begging God and everyone around you to help you be miserable.

To change this you need to build your confidence up, change your thinking style, change your perception about yourself and others, basically alter your perception of reality.

Keep it as simple as I am nothing but a magnet. Give into the fact that you are your **iGod**, you are a spiritual being. Treat yourself like a video game character that can upgrade your armor at any time and you don't have to do anything to get it except think about it. Your confidence and Conscious mind is your armor. The first thing to do to build up your Confidence is to remember the example of the atmosphere being Earth's "Conscious mind" or defense. If Earth had a weak Conscious mind that faltered and got insecure Earth would be bombarded by tiny tiny particles and comets killing us and nature. So take building your Confidence and Conscious mind serious.

No matter if you are unhappy with your figure **right now**, fall in love with yourself and who you are. Who cares what anyone else thinks (parents, friends, or randoms) **it only matters what you think about yourself**. If someone calls you ugly its not what they said that upsets you it is your own personal thought that starts to scrutinize and beat up yourself. You are your own worst enemy, you are your only enemy unless it comes to physical contact which most of us don't encounter. So come to the understanding that I'm controlling feeling shitty or feeling happy not the outside world. Don't get conceded or arrogant with this because than you'll be back to square one. The last 2 things that are needed for a good Conscious mind defense is knowing and believing that your parents, God, and Jesus love Every single thing about you. Don't worry about what your friends think they will come and go. Focus on you being happy with you, God and Jesus being happy with you, and your parents being happy with you. These are the only things that should matter to you and your defensive, confident Conscious mind.

Now it comes back to what we want our **iGod** to be. We all want to be a **Proton** and be happy and have fun; we all can be. But we have to want to be more than that and this is the hard part. We have to be like the **Nucleus** and be humble. You're probably saying, "Well the popular guy is an ass-hole to everyone and he still gets girls and friends. He's not humble about anything". I agree with this but when you don't care what people think about you, good looking and charismatic enough these rules really don't apply to you. Most of us aren't like this so we must make our Conscious mind the **Neutron** and our **iGod** (emotional charge) the **Proton**. This means that the happier and happier you become, the attraction or charge of your **Proton** will become stronger and stronger attracting more and more happiness and confidence. When your Conscious mind becomes the **Neutron** you won't care to tell people how happy you are or how cool you are now. Because trying to tell or show people how happy you are just means that you are trying to convince them that you are happy now, meaning you aren't satisfied with the fact that you are now happy and confident, which was your only goal in the beginning anyway. So if you feel like you have to try and brag about your new happiness and confidence you need to ask yourself, "Am I only happy with myself when others are happy with me?" No, who cares what they think. Think about your Conscious mind as a wall containing the positive (+) energy and preventing it from escaping. When you can master attracting happiness and confidence as well as being humble and keeping it to yourself, your world will transform before your eyes.

Going back to the popular guy his charge is powerful because he is confident and happy which attracts more people and more happiness. This constant **fuel** of happiness and confidence just strengthens and strengthens his **iGod**. He has become a **Nucleus** in any and every environment he walks into or is a part of. The strength of his **Proton** is so strong that he strongly attracts (pulls) or repels people. This goes back to what we talked about with my theory of **Spiritual Gravitational Pull**. People begin to revolve around them because they are attracted by that type of "positive (+) energy" while other people are strongly repelled because that type of "positive (+) energy", not their cup of tea.

So become like the **Nucleus** who is happy, confident, and humble. The happier you become you'll start to notice everyone (**Protons**, **Electrons**, **Neutrons**, and other **Nucleus'**) are all revolving around you. Eventually this won't matter to you because you are just focusing on keeping you, your parents, God and Jesus happy. Nothing else matters.

So start building your defense first, it is not hard, just convince yourself that you and everyone else loves who you are. Remember be humble about it. Then start your search for that long awaited positive (+) energy that has been waiting for you and everyone to tap into and utilize.

My suggestion is to begin building the defense (Conscious Mind) of your **iGod** by listening to your music and praying. Find the songs you listen to when you're down that you feel like are talking to you, about you, and talking about your situation. Let those be your defense and prayers to God. They are good reminders that there are others out there with problems and problems similar to yours. God will get a good read on those feelings and will start to help you out, only if you want him to help.

After you start building up your defense/confidence in your Conscious mind, **ALLOW YOURSELF** to feel and find happiness. You don't need a reason to be happy just like you have no reason to feel unhappy, most of the time we just are. We think we need a reason to feel happy which only makes us unhappy. So give into happiness and with your new confidence you won't be fazed and will continuously be happy.

Once again, start with your music to look for happiness. Next I would develop a good relationship with God and Jesus followed by fixing up your relationship with your parents, you can always start over with either (Unless your parents abused you or are part of the reason you are feeling shitty).

Convince yourself (like I did) when you pray that God has always and always will hear you. Then convince yourself that he is responding to you. Don't expect a voice, keep your eyes and ears open for odd sounds, movements, reactions from others, TV shows. The best time to listen for God is when you listen to music. Listen for him in the lyrics, he may be talking to you through the song. Be patient when watching and listening for God, it will take some time to read and interpret.

Every time you start to pray or want to talk to God, imagine that you turned on your **iGod** and have logged into your **Worldbook** account, you don't need music for this, you can do this whenever. The first time you log on you are probably thinking that God and Jesus are going to be mad at you. Well, probably from past sin and no apology they will be. But the thing they will be most mad about is your lack of effort to reach them or turning on your **iGod** to log in to your **Worldbook** account. So just start a conversation with God apologizing and explaining the bad things from your mess ups to why you feel so bad. Get the hard part out of the way. It won't take them long to change from being angry to extremely happy with the love from you. They will show love back and your world will transform before you even more.

When you come to the realization that everything and anything comes from God, good or bad, you begin to appreciate and find happiness in the tiniest things like your next breathe for example. It is that easy to be happy and I want everyone in the world to be happy. Because, truly it is that easy; we prevent ourselves from being happy. We are the ones who continue to judge, keeping segregation (Satan) alive here on Earth. We are the kerosene for these fires that engulf our World.

Instead of focusing on all the reasons why there can't be "Peace On Earth", why don't we start to focus on all the ways there could be "Peace On Earth". Let's start by fixing that **parallel** first and then everything else will fall into place.

God Bless the World. Amen.

2016

This is my final theory. This alone was the reason I finally decided to write this book. Honestly, this scared me into writing the book, I felt like it literally forced me into writing all of this down. Thank God I did because I think I would've been stuck in depression for the rest of my life had I not. Basically, **2016** is when I believe that Revelations or the "Apocalypse" will begin. Ironically by combining the simplest aspect of Science or mathematics, I came to this revelation you could say. The night before I discovered this me and my Dad were watching a show on History channel on how Issac Newton devoted a lot of time to figuring out hidden meanings in the Bible, similar to what I had been doing (which made me feel 100 times better, because I thought I was the only person to ever do something ridiculous like that). He came to the conclusion that Revelations would begin in 2060. The next day in music class I was thinking about that and this idea came into my mind. I had always been fascinated by revelations and had read it a few times. Here's how I discovered this:

In Revelations when John is "in the spirit" (in Heaven) he is standing before God and his Throne. In order of what he sees:

- 1 (God) on the Throne, but we know that God is the Holy Trinity (3).
- Next, 24 elders around the Throne.

- Next, 7 lamp stands in front of the Throne.
- Lastly, 4 beasts around the Throne.

So:

- (3) x (24) x (7) x (4)= **2016**

O.k. just coincidence but then I thought to myself, "what does 666 equal?"

So:

- (6) x (6) x (6)= 216

The reason I found this to be so real, was because I remember what was said about the number in Revelations, "Let him who has understanding <u>calculate</u> the number of the beast." So even if it's not true it's still a scary comparison. Also, going back to Newton's theory on when Revelations would begin, he believed that Christ would return 1260 years after the return of the Roman Empire. Rearrange the numbers you get 2016.

Also, the 2 witnesses stand on Mount Zion and preach for 1260 days. Rearrange the numbers you get 2016. The lady that is to give birth to Christ is taken away and hidden from Satan for 1260 days. Rearrange the numbers it is 1260. Other dates are used in Revelations such as 42 months which is 1260 days and 3½ months is also used which is 1260 days.

This I thought was kind of creepy and I will admit is kind of a stretch but could be part of it:

- 6+6+6=18 3+24+7+4=38
- 1+8=9 3+8=11
- 9-11

Going back to the first equation, it makes sense to see this as a representation of a date because it goes from 1 on the throne, God (1 day) to the 24 elders (24 hours in 1 day), then 7 lamp stands (7 days in 1 week), and finally 4 beasts (4 weeks in 1 month). I don't know how to explain why it is left off at a month and not finish at 12 months in a year. Regardless, these are measurements of **time**. So, it's safe to say that these numbers could represent the date of the beginning of Revelations.

To go further on this Revelations also states about the number, "he provides that no one will be able to buy or to sell, except the one who has the mark, either the name of the beast or the number of his name." So, this leads me to believe that the beast's mark will have something to do with technology being a part of the followers of the beast. This makes sense considering how advanced and how widely used technology is. Since the spawn of video games and entertainment, the advancement in technology is beginning to reach younger and younger. Kids as young as first grade (probably even younger now) are getting cell phones, playing xbox or gameboys. So, we can see how technology is slowly starting to reach to infants. I believe that the final technology that will do us in is the field of Nano-Technology.

So in summary, let's be thankful for the Earth we have been given, start spreading Water across the Earth, come together as a planet, and prepare for Revelations, which we all know is coming soon regardless if it's in **2016** or not.

Lastly, I never knew if I believed in the thought of destiny but after I made this last connection I did. My birthday is November 15th, 1990:

- 11 + 15 + 1990= 2016 (Holy Shit!!!!!)

That's when I freaked out and realized "I know why" you put me through it God. I finally found the meaning of the manic episode I had been so long looking for.

So I believe that writing this book was my part of the story in the "Book of Life" (my "upload" to **Worldbook** or the World itself), and had I not gone through and written this, regardless if it is accepted or not, I think I would have been miserable here on Earth and more than likely wouldn't of been accepted into Heaven. So my final advice once again is to listen to yourself, you know what you like and don't like and so does God. Follow where you feel your Heart is taking you, listen and look for God's direction and you will find peace of mind with yourself and will find Him here on Earth like I finally have. And if people find these theories to be valid and wonder how or why a kid like me could be blessed to figure this stuff out? My whole life I've been a good kid and was never really a "bad kid" you could say. But eventually I started partying and doing that stuff, just being a kid. I've always felt I was close with God and wondered if he had a problem with me partying and with me and a past girlfriend having sex. I finally just came to the conclusion that I love God and I can be forgiven of my sins and I'm sure God loves me too. And like I said before, I always believed I was supposed to something important for God in this world. I think God saw that and the fact that I embraced him when I was good or bad and looked on me with happiness and blessed me with this knowledge. So my conclusion is, is that I combined the 2 perspectives of being **good** and **bad** and found my purpose for myself and for God here on Earth. Most people are scared to think that way because we think we have to be perfect for God's love. Bullshit. I'm not saying just go sin and God will still love you. Seek God out, find him first, and keep him with you no matter if it's good or if you think it's bad in his eyes, keep him with you and he will love you no matter what. But, don't forget that there will be ramifications for your actions here on Earth that you can't control. I'm not saying you're going to hell, because if you except Jesus as your Savior you won't be going there. Think before you act, think with God.

God Bless the World. Amen.

"Everyone wants to change the world, but no one, no one wants to try."

- My Chemical Romance

Live by the Lord
Die by the Lord.

Live for the Lord
Die for the Lord.